FAITH, HOPE,

and

Shear Love

DIANNA BAUTISTA

Contents

Dedication

Jaa, for whenever your heart is ready
แด่ จ๋า เมื่อใดก็ตามที่หัวใจของคุณพร้อม

Foreword

BY KAYLIE HOUSEWRIGHT

In writing this foreword, it's hard to imagine being able to accurately describe this awe-inspiring, philanthropic woman, Dianna Bautista, in a way that I feel truly represents her goodness.

But I will try.

You see, I first met Dianna a decade ago in what I thought was her element, sitting in her chair on a set in LA, getting my hair done. We were two Southern California girls bonding over surviving unhealthy relationships and a mutual love for Chipotle. Not knowing that we would soon venture together on a life-changing around-the-globe journey—with only a twinkle of awareness that those shears would soon become her anthem of world change.

A weapon of choice used not to harm, but to liberate and educate.

As you will find, she has a way of making you feel comfortable the moment you sit down. Being a therapist, this is what I hope for clients to feel. As a beautician—and more so as just a person—this is what she does, naturally.

She will bring alive in your mind the reality of the

uncomfortable, nefarious crimes occurring in the world. But she will comfortably ignite a fire in you to create positive change. She will honorably share the stories of other resilient survivors in a way that urges your heart to compute them as your own.

And with all that she has experienced and in the trauma we've shared, it would be understandable for her guard to be up and her feet planted.

But no.

As you will read, Dianna did not just survive her past. She danced forward in commitment, healing those around her and helping them to grow with every turn she took and every leap to the new country she made.

As I have watched the chapters of her life unfold, I am astounded but not surprised by the masterpiece that has been created and continues to be written. While I live it as a supporting character, I invite you to bond with us and sit in her chair. Become a part of the inevitable live-action sequel.

These words are words you need to read, written by the strongest voice who is singing anthems of freedom for the voiceless. This book invites us into the flights and fights that will manifest your true element as a justice seeker.

So here is to becoming inspired at your very core. To transforming the way you think about yourself and the ways in which your current element is really just a foundation for how you can cultivate change and discover your purpose.

Dianna is a warrior. This book is now a weapon of choice, used not to harm, but to liberate and educate.

Enjoy.

Kaylie Housewright
Co-Founder of Free Rain International
Founder & Director of Injustice Response Training

About Free Rain International

Free Rain International is a global, faith-based organization that provides resources and initiatives to aid those enslaved, impoverished, and exploited. Our vision is to create options and opportunities for those rescued and oppressed in order to make positive and radical changes in our world.

Through global vocational programs like Shear Love, survivors and those at risk are given the opportunity to be educated and leave behind a life of poverty and exploitation. Injustice is inevitable. However, as we use our resources to pour out mercy, we believe that, indeed, justice and freedom will rain for all people.

Learn more about Free Rain and its programs at
freerainint.org.

1

The Underestimated

One bright California day, a guy named Mike strolled into my salon. "I'm here to sell you hair-cutting shears," he said.

Any hairstylist will tell you that you don't want just any scissors when you start cutting because it is *the* tool to our craft. The good ones are really expensive, but they ensure a quality haircut. But this guy wasn't just going to sell me great scissors.

Mike was going to change my life.

As part of the deal, he was advertising a program where I could trade in my old shears for a new pair.

"Well, what will you do with the old pair?" I asked.

"We send them to an impoverished area in South America where we teach women how to cut hair."

That immediately started something inside me. I loved that idea! "Can you call someone and tell them I want to come help?" I asked. "I'm into that idea."

Mike blinked. "What?"

I pointed to his phone. "Seriously. Call right now. Tell them I want to help teach them how to cut hair."

He looked shocked. "You want me to call to see if you can go to a third-world country to use your old scissors and teach people how to cut hair?"

"Yep." I nodded. "Right now."

So he called. A few days later, I had an interview and was accepted to go work with a team of stylists that were teaching eighteen to twenty women how to cut hair. All of the women in the class came from a world of drugs, domestic violence, prostitution, and poverty. All lived in the *favelas*, otherwise known as slums.

Society had told me my whole life that I was *just a hairstylist*. This is when I realized that I could do more.

And it didn't have to be that hard.

But You Live in America

While on that trip in Brazil teaching women to do hair, I met a woman named Victoria who had my exact same life story.

Literally, exact same.

She'd witnessed her younger brother being molested multiple times while she was growing up, just as I had experienced. Both of our younger brothers had been sexually abused by a close family friend, and both of us had witnessed it. She had also been in a very abusive marriage (as had I). Her father had left when she was young, under circumstances eerily similar to my father. In fact, Victoria and I were the same age, and our timelines for these events were the same. My jaw was on the ground as I listened to her tell me *my* story.

"The exact same thing happened to me," I said.

Victoria waved a hand dismissively and said through a translator, "Oh, come on. You're from America. That's where the Kardashians live and where Hollywood is. Everyone famous and rich lives in America. This couldn't have happened there."

My response came quickly. "No, that's not the way it is! Trust me, the Kardashians have problems too. They just have more money than the rest of us."

At first, I couldn't tell if she believed me, but the more I spoke, the more astonished she seemed. It was another big lesson—a moment of enlightenment for both of us. Although I came from the wealthiest nation in the world and she came from a slum in a developing country, we experienced the same things.

It's because we're all connected.

Despite all the things happening in the world, everybody has the same issues. We are more connected than we could ever comprehend. This is a big deal because it reveals one very important truth: we are not alone.

Victoria isn't the only person who's said this to me. "You're from America. You couldn't possibly understand."

But I do, because the human experience is everywhere. We are all experiencing the same thing in different places. That means the world is ripe for the harvest and waiting for laborers. There are so many places that we can help.

Even if we're "just a hairstylist."

Anyone Can Do What I Do Within Their Purpose

Throughout my life, I've had a lot of experience in the slums of the world. I've traveled and worked in Thailand, Kenya, India, Mexico, and many other closed countries throughout Asia. People call me the Humanitarian Hairdresser because I travel around teaching people how to cut hair and pull themselves out of sex trafficking. My project is called Shear Love, and we run schools that teach men and women how to do hair. We have classes in Thailand, Mexico, and Kenya, to name a few.

Our classes run all year long, taught by a mixture of local teachers who have graduated from our program and professionals who want to be part of our work.

Through my organization Shear Love International,[1] my team and I teach more than just the skills of a hairstylist or barber. We teach budgeting, sex education, personal hygiene, relationship building, and provide clients with counseling. We also teach them English. Basically, our job is to educate them on how to be an adult, which will keep them free themselves from the world of sex trafficking and exploitation.

The need for this is great.

But not everyone can—nor wants to—pack up and fly to a developing country, and live there. Nor is everyone meant to do what I do. We all have a journey, and all our paths go down different roads. That's a great thing.

But, in general, I think most of us want to create a better world. We want to *be* good and *do* good.

Yet . . . we're constantly discounting ourselves.

So much of it comes from our upbringing and the society we're in, whether we're in the US or the jungles of Thailand. People tell us how limited our power is. But the big secret is that we're only limited by what we allow ourselves to believe.

All of us are able to create a massive impact for good in this world. I call it purpose work, and we're going to dive into it right now. Purpose and passion and changing your life (and others) is what I want to talk about here. The truth is that most of us don't know our purpose.

Could you honestly answer these questions?

1. What are you here on earth to do?

2. What are you called to be?

3. Who are you called to be?

4. How can you change the world: first for yourself, and then for others?

Without purpose, we float. We feel lost. Adrift. Going through the routine. Our joy isn't as deep, and our sorrows feel *far* too deep. Maybe there's a sense in you that you're made for more—but you're not sure what. Or how to find it. Maybe you don't even know if you want to find it, you just know you want out of this funk. You want more.

I can help you.

You don't have to move to Mexico and start up a culinary school for single moms living in an impoverished village in order to find your life's purpose. That's certainly one way to do it, and if you're called to do that, I say go for it! But it's not the *only* way.

If you want depth and joy back in your life, finding your purpose will get you there. It will deepen your heart, enlarge your power, and create ripples that will never stop affecting you or the world. Think of it as planting seeds. They'll sprout and grow in their own time, and make their own beauty, but not if we don't plant them.

From my time as the Humanitarian Hairdresser, I've learned a few things:

1. Humanity exists everywhere.
2. Little things add up to big things.
3. Anyone can do what I do . . . within *their* own purpose.

Filling that empty part of your heart doesn't require you to go and live in the *favelas* of Brazil, thousands of miles from your family, and create programs to fight for the freedom of those enslaved by human trafficking and exploitation. That's my tactic.

But shucking off society's expectations of *who you are* and *what you can do* does require work. Those who are willing to work are the ones who move goodness forward in the world, both for themselves and others.

This book is written for those of us who want purpose.

We crave it. We crave more than what we have now, because we're convinced that this *can't be all there is*. We want to change the world for the better. But maybe we don't know how. We undercut ourselves, or let other people tell us we can't do it. This book is for those of us who are stuck and need to get out. We're not quite happy. We're not really serving.

We want more, but aren't sure where to find it.

In this book, I'm going to show you—the underappreciated, the underestimated—how to find your purpose. To help you do that, I've included questions within the chapters (with space to write down your answers) to get your thoughts going. Purpose work isn't easy. It's constant. Once you get started, however, you may find you don't want to stop.

Through finding your purpose, you can change the world. Like me, maybe people have been underestimating you your whole life. Maybe *you* have been underestimating you your whole life.

It's time to stop.

Because you can change the world, too, and it starts with finding your purpose.

2

When Society Discounts You

My parents are highly educated people who have worked incredible jobs. My dad was a city planner who has planned major cities, and my mom has degrees in English and Psychology and still works in special education today. But when I told my dad that I had decided to be a hairstylist, he rolled his eyes.

Yep.

Rolled. His. Eyes.

"You're too smart for that," he said and turned away. As if he hadn't just discounted the profession I wanted to invest my life into. "Find something else that requires more use of your effort and your brain."

Um, what?

So I turned to my mom. I'd been obsessed with doing hair since I was five years old. This shouldn't have come as a surprise to her. The dubious expression on my mom's face told me everything I needed to know.

"Dianna," she eventually said after she picked her jaw up off the floor, "are you sure?"

At the time, they wouldn't even let me cut *their* hair, so to them, there was something wrong with my plan. They thought it was a phase, which only made me want it more. Thankfully, my Aunt Nan talked some sense into my mom.

"Let her go," she said. "She'll flourish in her career. Plus, doing hair makes her happy. She needs to do something she's passionate about."

Regardless of their reaction, I pressed into my idea. Why couldn't I live a good life as a hairstylist? What was wrong with that? From the moment the idea sprouted, it seemed like people were against it.

As soon as I started beauty school, I realized it was more than just cutting hair. The work was *all* geometry and chemistry. I hated math and science, so it was challenging to do those aspects and still be creative with the actual haircuts themselves.

Being a hairstylist was more than I ever imagined, no matter *what* other people had to say about it. This was not a brainless job, and I was more determined to press against that stereotype than ever.

In fact, my cosmetology textbook was bigger than the Bible.

But I don't need to tell you this story, right? It's probably happened to you. From the beginning, people have been discounting what we can do in the world as "just a hairstylist" or "just a makeup artist" or "just a cook" or "just a plumber."

Shear Love even addresses this problem in our schools in Kenya and India. We teach the people in our class that they have to take themselves seriously because society won't always do that. Even if other people regard what they do as less-than, they don't have to think that way.

Our students worldwide know that when they have a customer in that chair, it is their time to speak into that person's life. To truly care for them. To make a difference in their day.

We teach them that they can support their family with dignity, empower themselves, and contribute to the beauty industry and the world. There seems to be a worldwide stigma about people doing trade work. Fry cooks. Mechanics. Makeup artists. Construction workers. Society makes it seem like we are unable to do anything else.

It's time to change that and reinforce our dignity.

What person doesn't feel better after a trim at the barber, or a cut and color with their hairstylist? When their garbage is out of their house? When their sink or appliances are working?

My brother has his master's, and I have a hair education. But our IQs are almost exactly the same. Our purpose doesn't define our intelligence, nor does it put a stopper on the impact we can have, or the depths of joy we can feel.

In fact, as "just a hairstylist," I've fought relentlessly for the freedom of men and women across the world enslaved by sex trafficking. We don't have to wait for society to approve of our intellect to make a massive impact in the world.

If you're waiting for someone to tell you you're smart enough, you're wasting time! Get to work. Find your purpose. Do some good.

You are smart enough! You are brilliant enough! You are *enough*. Go out and do it. I give you permission. And sometimes, that's all you need.

Permission

"WE DON'T MATTER."

Unfortunately, it's not just society that discounts us. *We* discount us. We think we can't do the hard thing. Whether it's our own insecurities, or years of being discounted by other people, or sheer overwhelm, I see this all the time.

The very first girl I met in Africa lives brightly in the back of my mind as a perfect example of the way we discount ourselves.

Before starting the beauty school in Kenya, I realized that the organization I was working with, Missions of Hope International, already had so many programs going that I honestly wasn't sure if a beauty school would work or not.

Wanting to hear from women in Kenya pushed me to do home visits, to hear about their lives and how we could best help. This helped me figure out what was needed so we were helping real people with real solutions.

One day, a social worker and I visited a woman named Jada. This girl lived in a nine-by-twelve-foot home with two young boys. The place was musty, smelly, and dirty. Flies spun slowly in the air or struggled in the dirt. Jada sat on the floor and gave us stools to sit on.

"I really want to go to school and learn braiding," she said, "but I'm terrified to leave my home."

Afraid? I thought. *If I were you, I'd be excited to get out of here!*

But then she shared her story, and my heart nearly stopped. A week before, she had been gang-raped by men in her neighborhood. She was terrified to leave her house because she was convinced that if they found her, they would do it again.

Swallowing back my compassion and rage, I forced

myself to get practical. I asked, "How will you support your children if you stay home?"

"I will do whatever I need to. Right now, I am a cleaning lady for wealthy Somalis. I want to do more, but I just can't."

"Okay," I said, "then let's go to the police! We can report this, find them, and make this right. Then you don't have to be afraid!"

She and the social worker both looked at me with expressions of tolerance. The social worker said, "This is not America, Dianna. This is the slum, and the police don't care."

"We don't matter," Jada said. "I'm a single mom with two kids. I'm viewed as a woman who sleeps around. Not everyone matters here."

At that point, I didn't know what to say.

No amount of protesting that *everyone matters* would make a difference. This was a different world, and it was a harsh introduction for me. To see the sorrow in Jada's eyes almost drove away hope.

Thankfully, the social worker encouraged Jada to keep talking. We found out that her husband had been killed during a political riot in the slums a few years earlier, leaving her alone to figure out a way to keep her sons in school and fed.

"Keep going," I said, hoping to champion her. "These men shouldn't control your lives, and your boys need more. They will see your strength and learn what it means to carry on."

With time and work, Jada overcame her belief that she didn't matter. Jada came to our beauty school, focused and ready to fight for a better life for her sons. Now, she is making five times the average daily wage in Kenya just by braiding hair.

The truth is that either society is going to discount us, or we are going to discount ourselves. But just like Jada, we can't let them control our future. We can't let them tell us what we're going to do next.

We are made for more.

There are so many stories of women around the world who feel like they don't matter. It happens everywhere. Not just young women starting out in the world, but anyone. In fact, I'm the founder and director of a global organization, and even I have been told I don't matter.

I have been called flighty, self-absorbed, unattractive, insensitive, and egotistical. There was one day in particular I was called mediocre, unintelligent, and a court jester by a person I absolutely respect.

That day, I learned a powerful lesson: you never really arrive.

In fact, you don't have to "arrive."

If I waited to be respected and supported by everyone, I'd still be in Southern California. Our schools wouldn't have been built. The people we helped would still be in sex trafficking—or dead from it. We don't have to wait for permission, approval, or even the feeling of "I'm ready."

Your purpose won't wait for you to find permission from someone else.

We can't wait until we "arrive" somewhere to fulfill our purpose. Purpose work is never truly complete in yourself or in the world. That means there's always someone who will discount you. That will take their issues and put them on you, as if you wanted them or asked for them. You didn't. You don't.

But they'll do it anyway.

We can't do good in the world if we're waiting for people to approve of us. Not everyone will. You can show up in your strength and power, and people will still try to take that from you.

Let them discount you, because their opinion doesn't matter.

But please don't discount yourself.

3

Purpose and Passion

Beauty school made me realize that, while people may say I've wasted my brain power as a hairstylist (something I adamantly disagree with), I actually would have wasted my *heart* power by doing something else.

To be honest, *heart power* is just another phrase for purpose, and that's what we're going to dig into now. Because you are here to find or amplify your purpose. Through that, you'll change your life, and probably everyone else's.

Going to beauty school was really a choice of passion. My heart was all in, and I had passion to spare. Thank God I went full force at my passion because my passion is what turned into my purpose. It was truly the first step onto this massive path I've been on. I'm so thankful I didn't let that go.

You're going to start, or perhaps already have, at about the same place.

Passion vs. Purpose

There's a constant tension between passion and purpose. You hear this kind of stuff all the time. You're encouraged to *follow your passion*, or you hear people say *this is my true passion* or *I'm seeking my passion.*

The problem is that passion is just energy, and energy runs out. You can't run or change the world on passion alone. Eventually, your passion will go out after a really hard day, or week, or year.

I've experienced my passion burning out all the time while fighting for freedom from sex trafficking in every part of the world. Being 10,000 miles away from family and friends, living and breathing the horrors of exploitation and abuse, means that burnout happens. It happens hard. And it happens a lot.

Passion dies and dwindles, and that isn't the kind of source to build your life on. You need something bigger. Something to keep you going when the excitement dies and nothing but gritty work remains on the road ahead.

That bigger thing is your purpose.

At the end of the day, purpose keeps us sustained. Knowing that God has called me to create a legacy and make a change in the world helps me push through the hard times. Purpose is the absolute foundation of our lives. It's so much more important than passion because it's the heart behind what you're doing.

Purpose keeps us going when the going is really hard. These days life gets really hard, even if you're in a wealthy country. Uncertainty. Abuse. Riots. Looting. Pandemics. Politicians. We are all living the human experience, remember? So we're all feeling it.

This is where purpose can pull you out of your rut and save you.

So how do you know what is passion and what is purpose? It's easier than you might think.

If you look back on your day and think, "Today was a good day!" then you know that passion was fueling you through it. You felt content at the end of it. Good things were happening! Energy is high!

On the other hand, if it was an absolutely horrible day, and you still want to fight, then you know your purpose is driving you. You're in the trenches. You're grappling with the monster. Despite struggling, you're still willing to fight when it's hard.

That's the power of purpose.

Just recently, our team worked with a young girl who was left on the streets of Thailand by her family. She struggled and was homeless. We picked her up and noticed she was *very* ill—both physically and mentally.

She was a teenager and American.

She had a history of running away. Her American mother (who we found on Facebook and who wanted nothing to do with her daughter) left her in Thailand because she didn't know how to take care of her. After her husband died, she felt she couldn't support her mentally ill daughter.

So she left her on the streets.

This girl was quickly picked up by people looking to exploit a minor. This, in the abusers' eyes, was profitable.

When we found her, she was living in an abandoned building in horrible conditions. She had been alone and homeless for two years.

We cared for her with the hopes of getting her back to some functionality. She had never been to formal school, so we had to get her up to speed. We gave her math, English, art projects, and creative things to work with. While in our care, she told us about all the traumatic things that had happened during her childhood. From extreme physical and verbal abuse to street survival. She was literally taken advantage of day and night. The needs of this case left us in complete burnout.

That's where the power of purpose kept us going.

We were not equipped for this type of case, which meant the team had to fight. And we fought through a lot of hard challenges, as exhausting as they were, because we knew no one else was fighting for her. We worked with the US Embassy, which was amazing. Kaylie called in to do online counseling with her during the week.

Eventually, we repatriated her to the US, to a home where she can be cared for 24/7. She will no longer be destitute and abandoned.

Without purpose, none of us could have made that happen for her.

The Brightness in the Dark

To be clear, purpose isn't necessarily when you *don't* feel good. You can feel really good when doing your purpose. I mean, how fulfilling is it to keep going regardless of how bleak the outlook?

Purpose is brightness amidst the pain, anger, and hurt of daily life. Purpose is what you're fighting for.

For example, we worked with another local organization and busted a pedophile ring in Thailand (which was the best thing ever). In the months leading up to the appropriate arrests, while reviewing the details of the situation, I sat there thinking, *This is disgusting and horrible, and things like this should never happen to seven-year-old girls. Ever.*

Even though it made me physically sick, I could not wait

to get up the next morning and continue fighting for their freedom.

Fighting for freedom is why I'm here. It is my purpose. My fight to fight.

But that's *my* purpose.

Not everybody can do my purpose work, because your purpose may be elsewhere. Your purpose may be raising your children to be lights in the world. Making other people feel beautiful through your talents. Enhancing your marriage. Helping other couples enhance theirs. Fighting poverty in your home state. Supporting political candidates who want to do good in your community. Teaching grade-school kids and providing a loving environment they don't get at home. Raising money for humanitarian causes. Taking a homeless person to lunch and talking to them about their life, because they often long for connection and community.

There are causes that need fighters everywhere on this planet—you're just reading about the one that I chose. If you turn away from this story grateful someone else is handling that situation, that's okay. Own that, because now you know that's not your fight to fight. Your purpose lies in something else.

Purpose can also create stability. So many organizations have come and gone in this kind of humanitarian work because they saw a great need, but lacked that intensity of purpose.

Purpose often drives intensity. For someone who has found their true, God-given purpose, there's a burning deep within them that means they'd do anything to fulfill it— even if people make assumptions about them.

One day, I went on an exploratory trip to consider part-nering with an organization in India. This place was very different from Pattaya . . . but equally as intense. We visited people and scouted out locations for a potential salon project.

Kelli and I walked single-file through a slum street (similar to the muddy, fecal-strewn streets we'd seen in African slums) with our guides, a husband and wife named Ryan and Aslyn. Aslyn led in the front, and Ryan took up the rear.

As we walked, a man grabbed Ryan. He signaled to Ryan that a little nine-year-old girl was for sale. From the moment he gestured to her, it was obvious what was happening. He wanted to show Ryan that she was a pretty, young girl he wanted to sell for sex. He saw a white man and assumed that's why Ryan was there.

Ryan shrugged the man off and kept going.

Seeing the expression on Ryan's face, I turned and asked, "Are you okay?"

He looked dead in my eyes and snapped, "No, I'm not okay."

When we arrived at our destination in the red light district, I said to Ryan, "I'm sorry. I didn't know what to say back there."

He relaxed. "It's okay. I get that it's a weird situation, but I will never be okay with a man trying to sell their daughter to me. They assume that's why I'm here, and it's not. I'm here to help free them. I'm not okay with the fact that they still assume I'm here to buy children. I will never be okay with that."

Despite the difficulty of facing that every day, he keeps going back.

He's there with his wife, serving in the red light district every single day. His purpose is to bring freedom to women, and he will fall on the sword every time those assumptions happen. People look at him every day and decide that he's there to pay for sex. They couldn't be more wrong. But his purpose lies deep inside him. He will not allow what they think to deter him.

Neither can you.

The call you feel stirring inside you? That's your purpose. Your purpose is what you're meant to do and accomplish in this world.

When your passionate fire diminishes for a multitude of reasons—disagreements with coworkers, a bleak living environment, an argument with your teenager—purpose is all that's left.

You might not know what your purpose is yet. That's fine! I didn't know what my purpose was when all of this started. I knew I was good at doing hair, but that's it. It's amazing how our purpose can unfold if we stay on our journey and pay attention.

Start paying attention.

Purpose work unfolds differently for everyone, so keep an eye out. Answer the questions below to help you have a better idea.

1. What feels good?

2. What are you drawn to?

3. What do you avoid?

All of us have something to give, and a purpose for being here. I stubbed my toe on my purpose.

In fact, it found me while I was investing in my passion.

Stubbing My Toe

A local community theater group called CAT was putting on plays with meaningful messages in my neighborhood in Corona, California. Cyndi was the director and one of my mentors, and I wanted to help. This group brought together children from all socioeconomic backgrounds and ethnicities to participate in a safe production that involved the entire family. Moms sold tickets. Dads built stage pieces. Kids decorated and performed in the production.

To help such a lovely effort, I volunteered to do the hair and makeup for the shows. It was work for a great cause!

Then 9/11 happened.

Like most of the US, I wanted to help. To do *something* in the midst of the horrors. But what could I do?

I was just a hairstylist.

So I decided to host a cut-a-thon to raise money. People would come, I'd cut their hair alongside other hairstylists, and they'd pay. All proceeds went to support what was happening in New York and Washington D.C. through the Red Cross.

That felt amazing. I paid attention to that and decided to try something else.

Next, I went to the hospital to cut the hair of patients undergoing cancer treatments. One in particular was my mom's friend, Barbara, who'd had a significant impact on my life. Serving her *also* felt good. My passion for hair kept me growing.

A short time after, my younger brother, Vince, successfully went to trial (with eight other men) against the man who had sexually abused him throughout his childhood. As a result of my brother's courage, the perpetrator was sentenced to 150 years in prison.

At the same time, my marriage was in the gutter. Despite feeling victorious for my brother and the other survivors, I was falling apart inside. I had fallen away from church for a long time as a result of my brother being abused, but was slowly coming back.

Many parts of my heart were bruised.

Ashley, my brother's then-fiancée (now his wife and the mother of the cutest children on earth—and that fact is not up for discussion!) had just returned from Africa, where she went on a short-term mission trip with our church. When she saw how badly I felt, she said, "Come to Africa with me, Dianna. You need to do this."

What the heck? I thought. *What am I going to do there? Well . . . I might as well go. It's as good a time as any.*

So I went.

OUT OF PLACE

Fundraising for the trip happened like a piece of cake. All the money I needed came in before it was due. In fact, it was almost *too* easy. At the time, I figured if it's God's will, it's God's bill! He would make it happen!

And it happened.

So I just kept paying attention.

When we landed in Nairobi, I stared out my window as a giraffe walked by the plane on the runway. It stared at the airplane as if we were just another animal. I couldn't believe it. The feeling of having landed far from home swept through me.

What had I done?

We stayed in a hostel-like hotel the first night and got up early the next morning to start in the slums of Mathare Valley.

While there, I had a moment of pure shock.

I am standing in one of the poorest slums on earth, I thought, looking around. *I could not be more out of place right now.*

During orientation, they told us that we'd walk through the slum doing home visits. "Visit someone's slum house," they said. "Talk with them. Ask them what they need. Prayer? Food? Share with them."

What the heck am I supposed to share with these people? I thought. *I live in LA, in Southern California, twenty minutes from Disneyland and thirty minutes from the ocean. I don't know anything about this world.*

My friend Sid nodded with determination. This wasn't his first visit. "I'm doing it," he said. "I'm going to talk to them. Come with me, Dianna."

So I went with him.

While in a slum house, he sat down, grabbed a woman's hand, and said, "God loves you. I want you to know that. No matter what you're going through, He sees you and hears you, and He knows. Make your problems known to Him. He's listening."

Her face lit up. "I believe that," she said. "I absolutely believe that."

When we walked out of her house and started down

another row, I paused. A bunch of women sat together near a slum house, cornrowing a girl's hair. A hand-painted sign on the side of her house said, *Salon*.

"What's going on here?" I asked the social worker who was with us. "Is there a local beauty school that they learn from?"

"There's no beauty school here," she said. "People look at them like they're crazy when they try to leave here, because they're from the slums. There's no education for them there or here."

That's when a lightning-bolt strike hit my brain.

These were the women I needed to help.

I leaned into that thought, which eventually led me to stumble on my purpose. Notice that it didn't happen right away. Years fell between that fateful Kenya trip and where I stand as a nonprofit director now. Those years wouldn't have happened if I didn't have passion, and if I didn't pay attention.

You can't overthink purpose work. Don't second-guess yourself. Just keep going.

Of course, sometimes purpose and passion can be as simple as data. If you're the kind of person who doesn't really have a compassionate streak or do the "feelings" stuff all that much, you still have purpose.

That's when data can be your best friend.

A LOGICAL PURPOSE JOURNEY

Kristi is a mentor of mine who I really look up to. We went to church together, which is how we met. She has twin daughters, and one of them has served with me at Shear Love as an art therapist for our first beauty class. Kristi runs a foundation named *Inspire Life Skills* that focuses on housing kids who have aged out of the foster system and teaching them how to be part of a family.

One day, amid a heavy situation happening with one of my students, I asked for her advice.

She immediately said, "You need to do this, this, and this."

My jaw dropped. "How did you come to that conclusion so quickly?" I asked. "How are you not hanging on to the emotions of this situation here?"

"Because I'm not compassionate."

You could have knocked me over with a feather.

"Of course you are!" I said. "The amount of work you've done and the transformation I've seen in the lives of those you've helped . . . you are compassionate!"

Kristi shook her head. "Not at all. I'm righteously angry at the data. That's different."

Despite the nature of her work, she's correct. Kristi is not a compassionate or emotional person. When she started hearing the terrible statistics about children who age out of foster care, she thought, *We gotta do something.*

"I saw those facts and was like . . . nope," she said. "That can't happen. It had nothing to do with feeling sorry for them. I wasn't taken by any one emotional story. I'm just not like that. I don't think that way. I don't start crying at commercials. With sad stuff, I usually think, *Get your life together.* But with these people, it was clear to me why so many of them end up on the street. They had a bad hand dealt. That's something we can fix."

Her approach to her purpose was logical, not compassionate.

Yours can be too.

She figured, "We have to make a family for these people. We need to create a structure."

Now, she has six supportive homes for those who have aged out of foster care and need to step into adulthood. Each person signs a contract before they enter so they are clear on the expectations—like weekly chores and other responsibilities.

What I love about Kristi's story is that she found her purpose on a logical journey rather than an emotional one. Kristi doesn't care about sob stories. She wants to know what they need and what needs to be done.

While most people go on an emotional journey, some don't. That's fine. Kristi is still a major contributor, and she bases it all on data and facts. If you're one of those people, you're welcome here too.

FINDING YOUR PURPOSE

This book was written to help you find or realize your purpose, then take action on it. When more people discover their purpose, their impact on the world increases. We're happier. Our families are happier. Then the world is happier.

We create better change, have more joy, and deepen ourselves through purpose work. It is the foundation of lasting change. Finding ourselves and changing the world will happen when we know our purpose, use our passion wisely, and trust in God.

Still, chances are high that you're not a hairstylist like me.

Maybe you're a plumber or a chef or a teacher. You shouldn't head off to Cambodia to start a cosmetology school if your greatest passion and talent is teaching math. The opportunities for us to find and flourish in our God-given purposes are endless.

Consider a chef. A chef has been specifically trained in mastery of certain things. They should use their skills as a *chef*, whether that means cooking in a restaurant that makes enough to care for their family, starting a café where half of the proceeds feed the homeless in their community, or initiating a vocational culinary school for people in need of opportunity.

It's all about finding your niche.

Start with your passion, and then you will find your purpose within it. You may even stub your toe on it, like I did. Your passion can inform your purpose, but remember that purpose is the heart of your work.

Now What?

So . . . how exactly do you find your purpose?

Start by asking yourself this question: *What am I passionate about?*

Of course, that makes it sound easy. It's not. Finding your passion is a bigger thing than a lot of people realize, because many of us don't feel passionate about anything. Maybe that's you. You might think, *I don't feel excited about anything, and I never really have.* Maybe you haven't found it *yet*, but the days are still ahead of you.

I've got your back.

Below, I've listed questions to help you figure out what lights you up. Start there. Answer the questions. Pay attention. Talk to some of your friends or family members and ask for their honest feedback. Dig deeper until you find the thing (or things) that have you so excited you don't want to stop talking about them.

So, let's get started.

First, use the questions below to take a hard look at your

passions. Write down the answers. Take time to think this over.

Go on a walk.

Explore it with your spouse or best friend.

Take this seriously—because it is the foundation of your purpose in this life.

1. What can you do?

2. What are you really good at?

3. What do you already know?

4. What do you want to know?

5. What fires you up?

6. What brings you joy?

7. What makes you sad?

8. What pulls on your heartstrings?

9. What makes you happy?

10. What could you do every day?

11. What change do you want to see in the world?

12. What could you talk about without stopping?

Once you identify your passions, pay attention to where they lead. If your passion is working with your hands to build electronic gadgets, how can that change the world? Can you teach others to do it? Can that change their lives?

Can you change your own?

If your passion is helping other people, narrow it down further. Do you want to do life coaching? Assist those who are sick?

When you know your passions, you're halfway there. You just need to find the purpose that simmers beneath it.

You may not figure out your purpose with just these questions. You may establish your passions and then nudge yourself to your purpose—that's fine. This isn't something that happens overnight.

But if you aren't intentional, it won't happen. Pay attention now. Engage in the things that you love, and search for the purpose that underlies all of them.

At Your Crossroads

Your purpose and passion may stew in your head.

Or maybe you know *exactly* what it is already! Even if you don't have your specific purpose, you have a better idea of how to find it. Or what to pay attention to.

Regardless of whether it's all figured out or not yet, the next step is knowing what to do now.

You might be thinking, *I can't just go to India! I have a life and home here. So, where do I start?*

You are not alone.

This is a conversation I've had often. Instead of thinking about what you can't do, think about what you *can*. What can you do in your own community? You can raise awareness. You can start talking about the things that you've seen and experienced. You can get people on board with your passion. Just start *talking* about your passion. See what happens.

Chances are good that right now you're already living your life and doing your thing. Maybe you are married and have kids. You run a salon. Or you teach at a school. Family responsibilities keep you anchored to one place, or maybe tremendous debt keeps you beholden to a job you hate.

If your passion is building wells for families in Africa, it may seem impossible to leave your life here and make an actionable difference there.

Guess what?

It's not impossible to pursue that as your purpose.

In this chapter, we're going to talk about how you make your purpose happen. We will find your next step and restore the missing piece in your heart. Here are a few key things you can do right now to start acting, and moving slowly toward your purpose.

1. **Figure out your talents.** Make a list of your talents. Be *honest*! Don't sell yourself short. It can be as small as sketching flowers and as big as building houses. Having compassion is a talent. Looking ahead to the future is a talent. Those can be massively helpful to your purpose. Talents can surprise us and others. Own what you're really good at, then step back and ask yourself, *How can this contribute to making my purpose happen?*

2. Act where you are. Think about what you can do in the place that you're at. I understand, you may have kids, a family, or responsibilities at home so you're not able to just pick up your entire life and move. But what *can* you do? Can you contribute to a cause? Do a fundraiser? Make dinner for a friend in need? What are some other things you can do to serve?

3. Start small. Imagine you're a makeup artist. Have a day where anyone can get their makeup done and half of the proceeds will go to your favorite anti-trafficking cause. Have flyers and information set up at your event, and share with people why this fundraiser matters. Purpose work doesn't have to be huge. What small thing can you do right now to contribute?

4. Speak up. Tell people about your passion and purpose. "This is what's going on in the world," you might say. "You need to notice." The clients I had coming in for color, highlights, and haircuts were with me for up to three hours. So I'd talk to them about my purpose: fighting for people's freedom from trafficking. They listened. Then they acted. Many still support my work today. How can you speak up and speak out from right where you are at?

5. What's stopping you? Who said you can't do this big thing or a little thing? If a specific person said that, who the heck are they and what makes them right? What makes them right about you? How do they know you better than you? Figure out what is behind the voices that tell you no or discount you in your own head.

6. Be willing to clean toilets. I *still* clean toilets if they need to be cleaned! Sometimes, the best causes need people to show up willing to do the work. Often, that work isn't easy or desirable. Maybe you won't be leading a specific cause or event, but you can work at it and support those who are leading. Willing hands make world change possible.

7. What things are you saying no to that could be keeping you from your purpose? Sometimes we're afraid of something because we subconsciously know how powerful it could be. Are you holding yourself back?

I'm your friend here, so I want you to know you *can* do this. Keep in mind that there are families in parts of the world that don't have indoor plumbing, which means they have to walk far to go to the bathroom, they don't have a place to wash themselves or a place to cook their food, and ultimately, they don't have clean drinking water.

In more developed countries, we can simply turn on a faucet and immediately have clean water. Like that hilarious meme that circulates around every now and then, we even poop in clean water!

We have so much.

Which means we have so much to give.

Often, when I encourage people to follow their purpose, some people are immediately self-defeating. They say, "Since I can't, I might as well not. I have kids. A partner. A job. What difference could I make?"

But if you're meant to do something, you just are. Period. The finances will come, the time will come. Turn your focus to your purpose, and you'll find a path. There are things you can do right at home. Push good ideas out to your social media instead of talking about a celebrity's new weird baby name.

Rally around your good ideas rather than others' negativity.

If you want to start building wells for families in need of water in Africa, take that small first step. Type *wells in Africa* into your browser, and start there. What do you find? Does this create a next step for you? Can you generate money to give to a trustworthy company?

Amazing things start from surprising, and sometimes small, circumstances.

SEWING FREEDOM

The COVID-19 quarantine began in the red light districts of Thailand at the end of March 2020.

When the COVID-19 quarantine order was issued, we felt a lot of emotions. We had been praying for that kind of thing to happen in this city for *years*. We've wanted the red light district to close, even if we had hoped for better circumstances.

Dayspring Foundation and Tamar Center (other organizations based out of Thailand that we partner with often) met with us to discuss what to do. At that time, thousands of women were out of work and needed to support their families, so we all knew we had to figure something out.[1]

For 5 years now, I have wanted to teach sewing and knitting classes, but didn't know how to sew or knit. However, I knew a few people who did. That's when I realized that COVID-19 had created an opportunity we could jump on: a textile school. But that meant we'd need supplies. Not knowing how to fund this idea, I said a prayer and said, "Amen." Less than a few minutes later, Missy from my church called me.

"Hey, Dianna. We're concerned because we had to cancel your annual fundraiser over COVID-19. Are you doing okay? Do you need some financial help in the meantime?"

"As a matter of fact, we do," I said. "We want to start a knitting and sewing school for the women who need work now that the red light district is shut down. Can you help us with funding?"

They immediately stepped up and sent us $1,000 to pay a teacher and buy the supplies we needed. Without those who contributed to that $1,000, even if they only gave $20, we could never have started this school.

How's that for little things creating massive change?

One problem done! On to the next. We needed a teacher.

Fortunately, we had a beauty student, Channa, from the previous year. She was good at knitting and crocheting. I called her and asked, "Can you come to the school and teach some girls how to knit and sew? It will give them a way to make money so they can feed their families while the brothels are closed. We can pay you for teaching them."

Channa said, "Yes! There are a few friends I used to work with in the red light district. Can I bring them?"

"Heck yeah, girl!" I cried. "Bring 'em!"

After that, we went into the streets and met up with women who were trying to make money for their families. We handed out condoms and invitations to a sewing program that we decided to try out.

Three days later, the school started with five girls.

At the end of the first week, we had eleven girls. After two weeks, we had eighteen. After a few hats were made, we took a bunch of pictures and posted them on Shear Love's Instagram with the following message:

Due to COVID-19, thousands of women in Thailand have been displaced, leaving them on the streets with no way to provide. The only way they were able to make an income to support their families was to sell themselves for sex.
Because of the recent lockdown of the red light districts, they have been left without a way to feed their children. Thanks to our partners at Crossroads Church, we have started a pop-up knitting shop for these women to earn income.
The women we are serving are receiving an education in

> *sewing, learning English, and having spiritual mentoring*
> *and discipleship. Each of these hats are being made just*
> *for you with Sew Much Love!*

Within three days we'd sold thirty beanies. In a week, we'd sold sixty. Two weeks later, we'd sold 140. By the end of the first month, we'd sold more than 200.

Nine of those girls asked to stay with our school once the quarantine was lifted, so they didn't have to go back to the red light district. Two of them were girls ages sixteen and seventeen.

When we started it, I had no idea if the sewing school was going to work. It was just an idea. But I put it out there. Started to ask. Sent out flyers. Let others support our idea to provide a better life for these girls. It centered around my purpose of fighting for freedom from sex trafficking, and the path manifested itself.[2]

This can happen for you, too.

The Harvest Is Plentiful

If you're still uncertain whether you can make a difference in the world, even with a small idea, may I lovingly remind you that the harvest is plentiful, but the laborers are few. Nine women in a sewing class in Thailand may sound like a drop in the ocean, but the ripple effect is much greater.

Those are nine women who don't have to return to sex trafficking. Nine women whose children will have a better life. If they each have two kids, that's eighteen kids who can then go on and change the world in better circumstances than their parents started in.

Maybe you, in starting small, will only reach one person.

Smile at one stranger. Donate $10 to a cause aligned with your purpose. But the most powerful thing is that you started. You did something.

You'll continue to do something.

Any of us can change the world one drop at a time.

WE CAN'T DO THIS ALONE

Sometimes, it may feel like there's just *too* much work. How can we ever do it all? This overwhelming feeling is really easy to come by, and it happens often in purpose work.

Kaylie, my partner in anti-crime, woke up with me in Kenya one day and immediately started to scream. We both had bedbugs! Our faces were covered in red spots and bites. Even though I wore socks all night, I still had huge red bumps all over my feet.

That day, we were giving a self-esteem seminar to middle schoolers, which was just perfect. Our horrible outward appearance allowed us to realize how important inner beauty—and talking to these girls about it—would be.

Ogre appearance aside, we gave a seminar to 300 middle-school girls. For over an hour, these girls asked questions about sex, such as *what's the difference between consent and being raped* or *what does it mean when . . .*

It was clear none of them had any sex education. We weren't even sure if it was appropriate for us to be answering those questions, but clearly no one else would educate them. So we gave each one a piece of paper and asked them to write down something they needed to talk about. They also wrote their classroom number so we could come talk to them individually.

Every girl wrote something down.

We sifted through all 300 notes with tears in our eyes and heavy hearts. Things like *my uncle has been raping me since I was five, and I don't know how to tell my mom* and *every time I go home, another kid in the neighborhood comes over and molests me.*

Almost all of them had to do with sexual abuse. Each one was horrific. The worst ones didn't have names on them, so we couldn't talk to them, and we weren't even able to visit all of them that day. It was unbelievable that there was that much violence happening in these 300 girls' lives.

Overwhelm crashed over me like a wave.

"There's only two of us," I whispered to Kaylie. "We can't do all this alone."

Her grim expression indicated she agreed. No amount of trying to fix it would give us the time or capability.

"But we're gonna try," she said. "We're going to do our best."

We had to do what we could, and let the rest go.

Maybe I couldn't save all of them, but I could make an impression. A difference. Speaking with every girl we could was another drop. Another chance. Another life that could be changed so *she* could go and change other lives.

We spoke to every girl we could reach that day, but we couldn't get to all of them. We taught them about their worth. Told them the truth. Helped them know they could demand better. In the end, I don't know if we made a difference, but I didn't let that stop me from moving forward.

When we got home, we asked a dozen friends to write encouraging letters to each of these girls, and we mailed over 100 letters back to Kenya. Something so small as a letter made such a difference in these girls' lives.

The harvest is plentiful, and the laborers few. But those of us who are working are working hard, and we are making a difference.

Don't be afraid to join us, even in the small things.

5

Comparisonitis

Right now, it's tempting to feel bad about yourself, your passions, or your purpose. It's easy to compare yourself to other people or wonder if your purpose is silly or won't really make things better.

It's not silly.

It will make things better.

And stop it!

Don't compare. When you compare yourself to others, it only makes it harder for you to act out your purpose and change the world. To deepen your own joy and feel better in your life.

Some people are able to pick up their lives and move to a different country to live out their purpose. That's great! That's *their* purpose and *their* plan. God has a plan for us all, and it doesn't always involve you in a foreign country.

You're living your plan right now, just like the rest of us. We're all on a journey. That journey doesn't mean you have to live abroad or start a school to teach life skills to the underprivileged or serve the homeless.

If something doesn't serve your passion and purpose, it's not your path.

THE QUEEN OF PATTAYA

Nella is the founder of Tamar Center, an organization in Pattaya, Thailand that has helped hundreds of women get out of the brothels. Tamar Center has helped save lives for over twenty years. Many of our graduates are able to work for them after they finish our beauty school, to stay on a better path.

Nella is meek, wonderful, and personable (she doesn't know we call her the Queen of Pattaya—she wouldn't like that, because she's so humble, so don't tell her!). Despite that, the sheer power of what she has done makes even the idea of meeting her intimidating. Not only that, but her reputation precedes her throughout all of Thailand, where she is so respected.

When she walks in a room, you sit up straight.

The first time I met her, I was in a meeting with eleven other organizations similar to Shear Love. We came together to discuss how we could work as one powerful force in the area. When Nella walked into the room, I felt her strength.

Who the heck am I to be around her? I thought.

Later on, she sat next to me and said, "I saw on social media that you're going on a trip soon. Where are you going?"

"I'm going to Africa in a few days," I said with a smile. "We have beauty schools there just like what we have here in Pattaya. I'm going to check on them."

Her eyes widened. "Wait, what? You have other schools in other countries?"

"Yes."

After I listed the other schools we have in six other countries, she looked at me with her mouth wide open. Then she blinked, sat back, and said, "Wow! I'm so honored to know you."

I put a hand on my chest. "Me? You are honored to know *me*? Are you kidding? After all you've done in Thailand? That's crazy! I am so honored to meet *you*."

"The fruit that has been produced from your school here is incredible. To know that it's happening in other schools around the world astonishes me. I'm honored to know you."

Excuse me while I cry my head off, I almost said.

This story proves that we never see ourselves—or our mission—as clearly as we think we see others. Nella was a woman I had been intimidated by before even meeting her. I had silently compared myself to her. In that comparison, I'd decided I didn't measure up. I found myself wanting.

If I had let that belief really sink in, it might have limited me and my potential. I might not have pursued my purpose. When we compare ourselves to others, we rarely let ourselves see our own power for what it truly is. It holds us back. Nella's reaction to meeting me proved that comparing ourselves to others will only hurt us in the end.

You may have done this in the past. You might do it right *now*. Stop it! Don't compare passions or purposes.

Find your path, and get on it. Be proud to be there. Light it up with joy and your brilliance, because only *you* can light that path.

Your path is *your* path.

Own it, don't judge it.

6

Fight For Something

At this point, you probably know something about your purpose, your next steps, and who you want involved in that. Maybe you don't know everything. You may never know *everything* about your purpose, but you can think about a path.

You may even be thinking about how you can take small actions to head toward that purpose. Even if you're just working to make a donation every month or volunteer at a homeless shelter, you let those small things become big things. Through vulnerability, you can create and change your community. There are passions, talents, and interests that make you unique. Even though there are millions of women who all face similar circumstances, there will only ever be one of each of us.

The smallest donations count.

There's work for you to do in your community.

Now is the time to think even bigger.

Now it's time to fight for something.

Everyone needs to fight for something if they're going to have a purpose. For the women I've worked with in developing countries, their fight is getting food and clean water for their kids. They are fighting for something.

We can fight, too.

By instilling that fight in yourself, you not only make more good in the world, but you receive more as well. It's time to get a fire going.

CALLED TO FIGHT

One day, I was attending a leadership training course in LA that a friend had enrolled me in. My friend Kat Harris, aka The Refined Woman, thought it would really benefit me before I moved to Asia. I was paired up with my coach, a woman named Monica.

Monica was unassuming for a life coach. I tend to picture life coaches as CEOs in sharp suits or as someone with a successful start-up. But Monica, with her long, dark, curly hair and freckled skin was a dancer with a chiropractic business. I didn't know it at the time, but she would go on to give me some of the greatest advice I've ever heard.

While sitting one-on-one, she asked me, "Tell me more about why you are moving to Southeast Asia. I'm so excited about what I've heard."

As I explained my hopes and goals, she said, "I feel your weight right now. I feel the burden that you're carrying, and it's a lot."

"Yeah, fighting trafficking is a lot." For a second, I felt the weight, too. Then I forced myself to perk up. "But it has to be done. Who else is gonna do it? I have to go out there and do this. I feel very convicted in this, and called to fight. This is my purpose."

She gently nodded her head until I finished, and then replied, "I think you're looking at it from the wrong perspective. As you're saying this, I feel that you're literally walking into a battle. Guns blazing, fists up. That's not who you are. You're far too loving to run in, guns blazing. I feel like there needs to be a shift."

"On the other side of trafficking," I said, "there's redemption, freedom, and justice. That's what I love about this work. It's why I consider it my purpose."

She paused for a moment and thought. With reserved wisdom, she finally said, "That's it. You're not fighting *against* trafficking, you're fighting *for* freedom. You need to be fighting for something, because when you're fighting against something, it's much harder on you. It's harder to get people to be on your side."

For several seconds, I just stared at her, testing it out in my head. She was right. After I changed my narrative, all of a sudden everything felt easier and lighter. Trafficking is so vast and broad, whereas freedom feels more attainable.

It's positive. Refreshing.

Obviously, I am still fighting trafficking, but fighting for justice and freedom takes something negative and transforms it into something positive.

Answer below: What are you fighting for?

THE LITTLE PRINCESS

Sometimes when we fight for something, it's not that glamorous. Purpose work isn't always quick. The results aren't immediate. Sometimes we're just planting seeds that will grow into the next generation.

But without those seeds, nothing grows.

My friend Chaz does a huge outreach every year to encourage women to help build up their sense of self-worth. Part of that initiative involves giving out roses with notes on them to women in the red light district throughout Thailand.

Each lady who receives a rose also receives an invite to a party the next day. Chaz's movement hosts it with the goal to help these women see their self-worth and their true value. He plans this event on Valentine's Day, which is a *massive* day for sexual abuse. Rapes on Valentine's Day skyrocket in the developing world.

I've seen the effects of it, and it's horrible.

Chaz wants to change that narrative through his movement. So we started partnering with them and gave out hundreds of roses. Each flower included an invite to a delicious dinner that had other organizations involved. We always get beauty students as a result of this event!

In 2020, there were forty people handing out roses. While out, we stumbled on a seven-year-old girl who looked very sickly. She wore a dirty *Frozen* nightgown with Princess Elsa on it while she sold fruit in the red light district at Section 6.[1] Once I saw her, I knew something wasn't right. Immediately, I called some investigators we work with who pose as buyers to get information.

We tracked this little princess for a while to glean information and even bought her dinner. After dinner, one of our outreach workers, Dorothea, followed her. The girl went to the back of the pickup truck where the fruit was being distributed. Women working in the brothels of Section 6 told us she was there from 6:00 p.m. to 1:00 a.m. every day.

It was hard to be patient, but we continued to watch. We wrote up a report, but needed at least one organization to report this case in order to get the local law enforcement involved. While we worked with partners and reports passed back and forth, we waited with heavy hearts. Someone had to help that girl . . . but it felt agonizingly slow.

But we kept going. We kept working. We fought for that little girl in all the ways we could—even if it felt so inadequate at the time. Even if it came down to just paperwork, talking with authorities, and a lot of waiting.

Two months later, we learned she was being sold for sex under the guise of selling fruit. Thankfully, because we waited and took all the proper steps, not only did we save her, but we took down her trafficker. We busted a child-trafficking ring and freed six other young boys and girls who were forcibly being sold for sex by the same man.

The trafficker selling them was arrested, and the children are now safe.

Sometimes, when we fight, it's not pretty. Nor is it exciting. Sometimes, our purpose is the least glamorous thing we'll do. But that's when we know that we fight for the right thing. When you're ready to go back into it day after day after day.

It's the power of fighting for something.

THE HAMMER

During the origins of Shear Love, and when I started to tell people I planned to move out of the country, the fear of all that change crept in.

I knew I was called to go, but no amount of pumping myself up made it feel easy. One day, I started sniffling in church while thinking about the monumental task that lay ahead of me.

One of my friends, Jonathan, sat at my side. He slung a heavy arm around my shoulders and asked, "What's up?"

"Can we get lunch after this?" I whispered. "I need to figure some things out."

After church, we got into his little Smart car (that I always called the roller skate because it was so small, particularly for his 6'4" frame) and headed toward Chipotle. Once we pulled up, I instantly recognized a ton of people inside. I stayed in the car, staring forward, thinking I was way in over my head.

"I'm moving to Asia," I finally said. My voice shook. "I haven't even told my parents yet, but I know that I need to go, and I'm so scared."

Despite all my certainty that this was my purpose and my path, doubt still filled me. The warring emotions of uncertainty and excitement created chaos in my heart. I craved clarity.

Jonathan leaned back and casually said, "You know, I saw this interview on TV the other day about a woman who, back in the 1980s, was engaged to be married to a doctor. Both were successful. They'd planned a really great life.

"But she felt something pressing on her to leave England because she felt that women needed her. She was like, *What? I can't.* Eventually, she ends up telling her fiancé a month before the wedding that she felt like she needed to leave England to help women suffering from violence. 'I need to go, and I want you to come,' she said to him.

"'Uh, no,' he said. 'I'm not going, and neither are you.' They ended up ending their engagement and called off the wedding. She traveled all over Europe and was able to help all these women out of horribly violent situations and forced prostitution.

"Years later, the BBC interviewed her and asked, 'You had it all with an amazing guy. Your life would have been comfortable. Why did you leave?'

"She said, 'I had a vision before I left. I saw a carpenter on the top of a tall ladder. He picks up a nail, puts it in the perfect place, and reaches for his hammer on his belt. But it's not there. He can't let go and miss the perfect spot, so he takes off his shoe and hits the nail in with that.'

"She said to the BBC, 'I'm the shoe. Someone else was the hammer, but they said no. They may have done a far better job, but I was willing to go.'"

My jaw dropped to the floor. Jonathan's eyes pierced me, and he said, "Dianna, you are the hammer. Don't let the shoe take from you what God has called you to do."

An overwhelming feeling of fear swamped me right then. I stared at him, utterly speechless.

His story made me feel like I was on my way to something so huge that I wasn't ready. Despite the fact that I had done a series of leadership trainings, did speaking events, stayed connected with my community, went through major therapy, and became very involved in my small group at church, I still felt inadequate.

But a feeling of conviction—of rightness—eventually followed. He was right. I *was* the hammer. And as the hammer, I wanted to be mentally, spiritually, and physically strong. I wanted to be a sledgehammer, not a weak, tiny rock hammer.

I still feel the same way today.

7

Find Your Community

Fighting for freedom from human trafficking isn't a fight that I could do by myself.

No one could! It would be impossible. There are millions of people enslaved today. More people are enslaved today than ever before in history. If fighting for the freedom of everyone caught in the global sex-trafficking web were on my shoulders, I'd bear the weight of more than 30 million people. In Pattaya alone, there are estimated to be 100,000 sex workers.

That means I get to work with an amazing team that helps me run this organization, because none of us should do purpose work alone.

With every issue the world faces on a global scale, we can't expect ourselves to be "cowboys" about fighting for better. You can't rally up, get on a saddle, ride into an endless desert, and think that you're going to make it out there all alone. You're not doing this by yourself, which means that finding your community is the most essential thing next to Jesus. Your community is key to doing this work.

After years of working in this field, I've found that a lot of people feel alone in their convictions—whatever those convictions are. Some of us tend to feel a huge weight on our shoulders that's impossible to lift alone . . . but we try anyway. That's ridiculous. We can do so much more together than we can alone.

Whether you want to support a cause that aligns with your purpose or create one, finding your community is key.

SURROUND YOURSELF WITH THE RIGHT PEOPLE

From the time I was five years old, I would steal all my mom's Paul Mitchell products so I could style my dolls' hair. Stephanie, who I've known longer than I've known my younger brother (for over thirty-eight years!) would let me do her hair.

In fact, I actually cut her hair with orange-handled kitchen scissors in her backyard on her brother's weight bench. Definitely the first, and most likely the worst, haircut I've ever done.

Regardless, she remained my lifelong friend and was one of my biggest supporters through my brother's trial and my divorce. We even became roommates after the divorce, which brought a new level to our friendship. She supported me in my wild missionary work and remains a constant in my life. I flew home from Thailand for five days in 2019 just to attend her wedding.

She is the right kind of people for me.

Now it's your turn to take a hard look at your life. Answer the questions below in the space provided.

1. Who is your Stephanie?

2. Who supports you unconditionally?

3. Do they challenge you to be better?

4. Can you constantly learn from them?

When it comes to living your purpose, author and podcast host Lewis Howes said it best: "If your circle isn't cheering you on, then find a new circle."

Who do you surround yourself with? Notice that this is different than just those who are around you. You can't choose your coworkers, right? You aren't going to get rid of your kids. Don't consider them in this question. Think about the people you allow to *speak into your life*. Those who help you make decisions need to be the best kind of people.

They are the people I want you to find. Be intentional about it. It took me thirty-eight years to solidify my community, so it won't happen overnight!

Of course, this may mean letting go of others.

It's okay to let go of people. You shouldn't feel shame, guilt, or condemnation. You have to focus on yourself for a moment and think, *If I'm going to be moving forward and serving other people, I need to make sure that I'm not stuck with a group of people who don't support my purpose and don't have the same vision and values as me.*

This isn't easy, but it is key.

Maybe a friendship separation has been something that needed to happen for a while, whether it's a spouse, friend, former romantic relationship, or boss. It's okay to lose people, especially if they're not good for you.

Or if you aren't good for them.

For example, if you have someone in your circle and they don't want to hear a word you're saying, then they don't have your best interests at heart. They may have their own things going on, or may not feel driven to support you in your purpose. That's fine. But don't stick around there, waiting. Find yourself a team that supports your purpose and your vision, as much as you support theirs.

This process might take time, and is always changing. New people come into your life, and other people go.

Create the community that you need to honestly change the world or even your home, because that can change the world too. In all the work I've done abroad, I have never rescued one person by myself. There has always been someone backing me: a team and my community. There's not one person that I've educated, rescued, rehabilitated, or reintegrated back into society alone.

No one expects that of you, either.

Here are a few MORE questions to get you thinking about who your true support team is:

1. Who are the friends that allow and encourage you to live your passions and purpose?

2. How do they support you where you're at?

3. Are you allowing the people in your life to live the life *they* were created for?

4. Are you holding them back from what they're meant to do?

5. Can you call them and ask for support, whether it's emotional, spiritual, or physical? (And are you doing the same for them?)

6. How are they good for me?

7. How am I good for them?

This isn't easy work. It takes self-reflection, breaking down pride, and a willingness to accept feedback. It needs to happen with yourself and with the friends around you. What we expect of others, we have to expect of ourselves as well.

Surround yourself with cheerleaders and be one for others. Don't be selfish when you seek community. Be there for them as an exceptional part of their community.

Your community should fuel you as you fuel them.

Be Vulnerable and Find Your Hype Team

Finding your community has a *lot* do with vulnerability.

Vulnerability isn't easy, but it is so important. Many people are afraid of vulnerability because they don't want to share and appear weak. But through your weakness, you'll find your strongest community, as well as those people who will hype you up when you need it.

During my divorce, I sat next to my wonderful friend Megan Foster in church every Sunday. (I call her my Foster sister and her parents my Foster parents.) Every Sunday, I sat with her and cried my eyes out. Every Sunday, she brought tissues and passed them to me. She wanted to take care of me in a way that I needed, and at the time, I needed someone to just sit there and pass me a tissue in my vulnerable moments.

She sat there *in* it with me.

Another friend of mine, Rose, listened to me cry while I was in the abusive cycle with my ex-husband. Rose and I met over twenty years ago at cosmetology school, and she always told it to me straight.

One day, while I cried on her shoulder, she said, "You can leave if you're tired of it."

"It's not that easy," I said.

"Yeah, it is. You're making it hard, but it's still something *you* need to decide. If you pack your bags, I'll meet you at the curb."

She was right.

I had to move myself. No one could move me.

No one can move you.

That took compassion on her part, and vulnerability on mine. When you share who you are, what you're doing, and what you're going through, you can not only get validation from the reactions of those you're telling, but you can find the right people to continue to support you. They can be your community.

But first, you have to be able to have *real* conversations. That may mean you are vulnerable with your story, or you allow others to be vulnerable about their story. The more vulnerable you are with other people, the more they'll do that for you. Then you can return the gift.

That transparency lifts you both up to fly a little higher.

Community is mutual.

FIND YOUR FRIENDS

Bear with me as I tell you about these incredible people —because there's a point at the end.

In Thailand, Stephanie Henderson is the financial director and administrator at Free Rain International, and she also runs a lot of the show as an admin in Pattaya. She is level-headed, logical, and creative, and she thinks out the details of everything. Stephanie even designed the class-room for our Sew Free students. That is hard to find all in one person!

I always say she is the string to my balloon.

Kelli is our lead beauty educator and the chillest person ever.[1] She is easy going, ready for adventure, and wants to jump into a photo whenever I need a model. She also makes sure our students get the best education. She's all about helping students get legal country certification (the Thai equivalent of a beauty license). She's methodical and gifted with hair cutting. She's an amazing friend who shares my passions and purpose and love for Indian food!

Dorothea is German-born and Oklahoma-raised. She is brilliant, very quiet, and speaks four languages fluently. She teaches English to Thai students and handles all of our videography and photography on the ground. There is a saying that still waters run deep. Dorothea is deep and still. She has the stamina to last. She is a leader on our outreach team.

Dorothea is everything.

Julianne is my hype girl, the color of sunshine, and forever cheerleader![2] She also is a leader on our outreach team and has been responsible for finding more than half of the women who have enrolled at Shear Love in Thailand. She is a visionary and a dreamer and will stop whatever she is doing to dream with me.

In the States, Brianna is on top of things and is incredible. She works at my home church and is a fighter for us through the Global Outreach department. She's on top of business and always gets us what we need. She's gorgeous, to boot, and makes sure everything is done with excellence.

Missy is also from my church. She is amazing, and we've both been through stuff. She knows when things are not okay and always reaches out at the perfect time. She is the kind of friend who has always been there, no matter what. Also, stunningly gorgeous.

Now that I think about it, all my friends are!

Rose and my first Stephanie are lifers and remain wonderful encouragers in my circle, decades later.

Kaylie, who needs no explanation, is my BFF and my person for life and partner in anti-crime, is my best friend in all my circles.

Of course, you may think, *That's great, Dianna. I'm happy you have such amazing, gorgeous friends. How does this apply to me?*

It applies in a big way!

I'm sharing all this to show that friends are key to purpose work—and you need them too! Each one of these women came into my life at very different times and seasons and for different purposes.

The Stephanies in my life I met at very different times, but they are both pastry chefs—which is just so random, but also so perfect! My first Stephanie I met when I was three, and my second Stephanie I met at thirty-five.

Very different, but both had perfect timing.

The same may happen to you, so pay attention. You bring in the best friends when you are *being* the best friend in return. You want amazing people who can support you—and who you can support. Having mutual passions and purposes isn't necessary, although often it's very helpful.

In your community, you need someone who recognizes when they need you. They also need to be there when you need them. That's often missing! Some people don't know how to put themselves aside to help someone else.

Does your community?

Do you?

These people have been there for me, and I've been there for them. That's what makes purpose work stronger.

One amazing thing to consider is that your circle will change over time. People may move in and out of it.

Together, it will be an all-encompassing network of people that's like a ball of entwined yarn. There is something so powerful about picking up people and adding them to your group, then pulling on them when needed.

It's okay that it changes.

Sometimes you hit it off right away. Sometimes it happens later. Whenever it happens, there is power in helping others, or allowing them to help you, as you both work toward your purpose.

Find Your Mentors

Mentors are an integral part of your community and your development. You want someone you can have tough conversations with that will lead you in the right direction. You need people who will guide you.

In the depths of despair during my abusive marriage, I turned to Pam. She's married to my pastor at home and always held a nonjudgmental space for me. I pleaded with her, "Please, tell me what to do."

She looked me right in the eyes and said, "I can't. You'll have to come to that on your own. You have to reconcile with yourself, and I can't make this decision for you. If I do, then one day you'll resent me. That means you need to find the strength in you. Only you know what is right."

That is the kind of mentor you need.

Someone who will guide you, not tell you what to do.

What Is a Business Plan?

Lisa Mitchison is the Global Outreach Director for my home church, Crossroads Christian Church in Corona, California. She's a huge reason I'm in mission work. I went to

Kenya with Lisa and her husband Ernie three times when they were team leaders of the trip. She and Ernie were both there when I saw the salon shack that spurred my initial idea.

One day while in Africa, we had just finished at a medical camp in the slums. At the time, we were doing a project called Bring the Light. We would work on roofs to create a skylight so they could get light in their shacks.

It's actually a needed thing.

At the end of the day, Lisa, who is much shorter than me, said, "I need to go do something in another part of town and need someone to go with me. Will you come?"

"Hey, I'm down for that. I'll be your bodyguard! Let's go!"

We climbed into the back seat of a car with the founder and director of the Missions of Hope International, Mary Kamau.

"We have a lot of extra money," Lisa said to Mary during the drive. "What do you need? Do you need to build a school? Open a medical facility? Help rebuild homes? What more can we do with this extra couple thousand? What does the community need?"

"For five years, all I've ever wanted to do is build a beauty school for the women who want to do hair but don't have access to quality tools or products or a teacher," Mary said defeatedly. "There are many things we need."

Lisa looked at me in total silence. I sat there for a second, eyes wide. Had she just said what I thought she said? Mary noticed and asked, "What's going on?"

"I'm a hairstylist!" I cried. "I've been one for ten years. I can help!"

After we returned to the hotel, Lisa said, "You have a lot of work to do, young lady. You need a budget and a business plan. Sounds like you better get started, because you have a hair school to build here."

I got back to my room, fell on my mattress, stared at the ceiling, and thought in a panic, "What's a budget? What is a business plan?"

Thankfully, my business administrator brother Vince swooped in as a mentor and helped me out. We submitted a plan to my church and received approval for $20,000 to start a hair school in Kenya.

Since then, more than 500 people have successfully graduated from this school.[3]

All of that came from a meeting I wasn't even supposed to be a part of, combined with the mentorship and encouragement from Lisa and Vince. Lisa gave me permission to fly with the idea, and I did.

She saw more in me than I saw in myself . . . and that is so important in a mentor. They see more than you see.

We need others to see us first sometimes.

THE POWER OF MENTORS

To help you see the best characteristics to look for in your own mentors as you do purpose work, I'm going to tell you more about my favorite mentors. Pay attention to their strengths—and what they've done for me—so you know what you need. Then you'll be able to better seek your own mentors out.

THE WITTY DUTCHIE

Fayanna Worrell is a Dutch woman who is six feet tall. She has the biggest hair that adds almost six inches to her height. She's hilarious, but she can drop that in a second to have very serious conversations that encourage action.

The ideal mentor.

She also hosts women's conferences internationally. In 2019, I attended one in Kenya with 1,000 women participating. While there, I visited our school, charted out new territory for other programs, and I spoke at this conference, thanks to Fayanna.

Fayanna has stood with me through everything for more than twenty years. She never belittles and is always there no matter what. I've never once felt condemned by her, but convicted to move to action. Together, we laugh through life.

She had a hilarious idea for us to start a hair salon that was also a coffee shop—she called it the "Sip 'n Snip." She's a comedian and only gets more beautiful with age.

She is also now on the board of directors for Free Rain International, and is the epitome of wise counsel.

THE SPICY MEXI-RICAN

Debbie is a spicy, fiery Mexican and Puerto Rican woman who looks way younger than she is and loves to get the party going.

All of my mentors are stunningly beautiful. Who they are and their love for people shines out of them like a beacon. Debbie doesn't disappoint. When she calls me, she says, "Mijaaaa! How are chu doing?" in the thickest Spanish accent that makes my heart flutter every time.

She is my biggest source of encouragement. When things are difficult, I message Debbie, and within one minute she is messaging me back with the prayer hands emoji. That's all I need, because I know she means it.

Debbie isn't one of those who says, "Praying for you," just to say it. She says it, and means it. Everytime.

THE HUMBLE KIWI

Leanne, or as we call her, Mama Lea, is the humblest human being who lives a stone's throw away from Hobbiton.

When she came to Thailand to be a house mom to our Injustice Response students, she actually applied to be a student. Of course, she was past the age bracket, but she really wanted to be a part of the program no matter what.

In fact, Mama Lea leads humanitarian trips for groups around the world. She has tons of experience, yet still desires to learn.

Her humility has been a focal point for me. The amount she has accomplished and still wants to learn pushes me to do better.

She is a forever student of life, and that's something I admire.[4]

Hopefully, through the lens of my mentors and what they bring to me, you can find your own. My mentors stemmed from my community. They are my friends as well. Remember the key ingredients here: Community. Vulnerability. Mentors.

These will take you into your purpose work. There are billions of people on earth, and all of us are experiencing the same things.

You're not alone.

FIND YOUR PARTNERS

Fighting for freedom from sex trafficking involves the unwinding of a complicated—and illegal—tapestry. It takes dedication, time, and support to reach the people who need us to rehabilitate them from the lives they lived and into better ones.

We could never do it alone.

That's why we have found and work with dedicated and intentional partners, such as Tamar Center (which I've mentioned before). Tamar is an organization that has helped hundreds of women in Pattaya. Thanks to our partnership, we work heavily with them to help our students and recruit new ones. Tamar works on cases and gives advice, and was founded by Nella (the Queen of Pattaya), who is a pillar of wisdom and someone I look up to. They just celebrated their twentieth anniversary, and they have helped us out through many situations.

We've found partners all over the world that align with our purpose.

These partners all give us support that creates greater success for us. Not only that, but we are able to work on our purpose through them as well.

For example, Grace Salon and Training Program is a newer program in the south of Thailand that was started by my friend Allie. We've helped and they have helped us in return. We provided them with a full beauty curriculum to start their program, and they translated that curriculum into Thai for us.

Dton Naam is an organization that works with men and trans women. The founder, Celeste, hosted a training for us on how to reach out to the trans populations with love and support.

Unfortunately, forcing boys to live as girls is common in Thailand—the parents of these boys will raise them to be women just to work in sex trafficking knowing they will bring a lot of income to the family in the future. They are referred to as *ladyboys*, which is the proper term to talk about people who are transgender in this country. Celeste helped us understand these nuances as we work with this population.

Working with partners has been incredible and has completely altered the way we're able to do our purpose work.

We're also able to help our partners. In Kenya, we're partnered with Missions of Hope International, which is the first school that I helped build on my own. Crossroads and I were able to provide them the funds to pay for the construction, tools, curriculum, teachers, and teacher training. To date, they've had over 500 graduates from that school. They've even been able to expand and offer advanced classes, and even a class in a rural area. They now have three different schools.[5]

1. How can you find a community to take you through your purpose journey?

2. Write a list of people you would like to be in your circle, be your mentors, and with that, people you can also help.

8

Failure Will Come

When it comes to fulfilling our purpose, we have to deal with failure.

The inevitable wall that you'll hit will come. When that moment arrives, you need more than passion to continue being effective. Maybe even more than purpose. You need something deeper and more solid that's always ready to catch you when you fall.

That comes down to two things:

1. A strong community.
2. A solid spiritual foundation.

We've already talked about the importance of community, so now we're going to talk about spiritual foundations.

It's probably not what you think it is.

This applies to anyone, particularly if you're working with people. No matter what kind of passion you have, life throws curveballs. Purpose work itself can feel like a burden to bear. If we don't keep ourselves centered, we'll never be able to help anyone else.

While in Kenya, a woman named Lillith attended our classes. Her sweet personality immediately endeared her to me. Although she always wore long clothing and scarves, I didn't think anything of it at first. Kenya tends to be a very modest country. We found out later that she was covering extensive physical abuse from her husband.

One day, she was twenty minutes late to school. I took her aside to give her my basic teacher lecture on why she shouldn't be late.

She nodded and said, "Okay. I'm sorry. I will not be late anymore."

At the end of class, she revealed to our Swahili translator some of the bruises where her husband beat her every day. That morning, it had hurt so badly she could barely walk to school.

This story doesn't have a happy ending, because she dropped out of the program and we didn't see her again.

That's exactly why I'm telling it. Failure is a huge part of purpose work. The only positive take I can muster is that she felt loved each and every day she came to class. I still pray that love stayed with her.

Not every story is happy rainbows.

This is why we need a strong spiritual foundation and a solid community to fall back on. We look forward to hope and find the silver lining. If we can learn to find the positive in purpose work, then we don't bail out.

A STRONG SPIRITUAL FOUNDATION

So much of your strong foundation comes down to consistency.

When I started this whole journey, I made a choice—a

very serious, intuitive choice—to step deep into my faith. It has been a source of strength for me many times.

For me, that meant I showed up at church every week. I made time to be with friends who would boost my faith. I found a community that encouraged my walk of faith and my vision for my life.

Your spiritual foundation comes down to two things: your self-motivation and your community. (See how important community is? I can't stress this enough!)

This goes beyond just *who* and to the *what*.

Here are a few questions to ask yourself, with space provided for answers:

1. What influences do you surround yourself with?

2. What kind of food are you eating?

3. What kind of music do you listen to on the radio?

4. What do you watch on TV?

5. What are you putting in your mind and your head?

6. What kind of people do you hang around?

Those things come out in your body as well. Plan to cleanse your whole palate when you start into purpose work. Break it down to the simplest things, and make them better. Building a strong spiritual foundation is about more than just prayer—you have to take it to the next level.

When I was in high school I loved rap. Like *loved* rap. As I listen back to those songs now I realize how demeaning most of those lyrics are to women and how divisive they can be. I can't believe I allowed those words to bury in my mind for so long.

Something you thought was funny years ago may not serve you now. Maybe you loved a TV show when you were eighteen, but when you see it now, you realize, *That doesn't make me feel good. It doesn't present people in a very good light.*

Get rid of it.

It's like Marie Kondo. Does this bring you joy? Clean out your life physically as well as spiritually! Most spiritually harmful things bring awful things to our minds. They don't bring joy. So it's time to Marie Kondo your brain.

Your house.

Your life.

Set very clear intentions. That may mean setting an alarm on your phone that says, *At this time, I'm cleaning my room.* Block time out in your Google Calendar, and keep it sacred. Don't put anything else there—then do things that enlighten you during that time block. Build your foundation by serving and uplifting yourself.

Read books that serve your purpose and community.

Watch an educational documentary.

Tell people you're busy.

This is your personal development and growth time. This will put you on the pathway that you need to be on in order to serve the world. In order to serve those around you better. Your true circle will respect your time and dedication to being your best self.

Turn to your self-discipline. If you don't have it, make it. Find it.

Start small with those things, and then build upon it. Make sure the people around you encourage you to be your best self, and you encourage them to be their best self. Eventually, it grows around you and into your whole life.

JUNE

June showed up the first day to our inaugural class in Thailand with a hangover.

She looked so adorable in her K-pop star outfit and fake braces that I couldn't help but like her right away. Still, that day set the tone for what would follow for the duration of that school year.

June showed up as the last to class frequently, regardless of my stern disapproval. Despite eventually implementing late fees, she would pay her fine and continue to arrive later and later. The other girls in the class were free, and happy to be out of that life. June couldn't have cared less! She didn't appreciate the safety, the free school, or anything else.

"Nothing is going on," she assured me when I asked —repeatedly.

As she withdrew further and further from the class, it was obvious that she was still renting herself to customers for sex. It's actually written in their contract that they cannot do that while in our beauty class.

I didn't want to believe it, even though it was obvious.

Finally, she began to miss multiple days a week. In their contract, they agree to miss no more than one day a month. That triggered the day I had dreaded.

We needed to talk.

My translator and I sat with her one day. "Do you really

want to be here?" I asked.

"Yes."

"Then why don't you show up?"

She looked down and said, "It hurts to get out of bed. I have so much pain and stress that it's hard to sleep or get out of bed."

"Why do you have all this stress? Let's talk about it."

"My mom needs money, and I need to work to care for her." She threw her hands in the air and said, "How am I supposed to pay my mom's debt? How else am I supposed to help her? This is all I have to give."

Her bomb-drop stuck with me for years. *All I have is this. What else can I give?* A similar question came to me from a girl in Kenya. *My children cannot eat unless I sell myself for sex. If I don't do it, my children will starve.* A girl from Cambodia vulnerably shared *I do this so my little sister does not have to.* For these women, their body is *all* they have to give. It's difficult for many of us with a Western upbringing to understand that sometimes all these women really have is their body.

That's it.

This cycle continues through the generations. They cannot get off this hamster wheel because it's the way it's always been. They don't know any other way, so they give up their body to serve their family. It's sacrificial.

At the heart of this, they are the heroes.

"You have such an important and powerful influence in this class," I finally said to June.

Her head jerked up in shock. "What?"

"You roll up late on your yellow motorcycle, looking mad, smoking a cigarette, and can still do a full head of cornrows in twenty minutes. You are the epitome of cool."

Even I—who had been doing this for years—was

amazed at how she made it all happen. Her 50% was someone else's 100%. If she really applied herself, she would make more money than she could even dream of.

I was taken back to the wise words of my friend Rose, who'd comforted me through my abusive marriage. Tears filled my eyes when I said, "This is my dream for you . . . but it needs to be *your* dream for you."

She put her head in her hands and cried. "I've never had anyone tell me that I'm important." Then she giggled. "I'm really uncomfortable right now."

"I'm uncomfortable too. Let's get through this together."

After that, she rode off into the warm sunset on her yellow motorcycle. I prayed all weekend that she would show up to school on Monday. She did—but then she skipped on Tuesday. A back-and-forth battle continued for the next couple of months before she finally quit altogether.

She came back and enrolled the next year. By this time, I'd stepped away from teaching and Taylor was her instructor. Maybe a new teacher would get through to her. Nope. June put all of us on a roller coaster of emotions all over again. One day, she asked to talk to me. We went to the office, and she said, "I'm pregnant. You'll let me stay in school, right?"

"Yes, of course. Do you know who the father is?" I asked.

"No, I don't."

"That's okay. We'll work through this."

Despite a new resolve to change her life for her unborn child, June continued to be absent intermittently. When the time came to have the baby, her water broke.

In class!

I couldn't believe it. The floor was all wet, and we panicked. No one had a car, so we called an Uber. June had a beautiful baby boy that she named Tay, after Taylor. I met her mother—who appeared to be a sweet older woman. She was pleased to have another grandchild. Partially because it meant that June could go back to work, which is a common belief in some impoverished communities.

Despite the anguish of leaving her three-week-old with her mother, June remained enrolled in our school. Within a couple of months, her previous behavior started again. She was back on the streets, pressured by her mother to make money to support all of them.

In disbelief, and at the end of my rope, I made my final offer. "I will be your customer. I'll pay you whatever you want."

"Teacher," she gasped. "You're my teacher, and I cannot treat you like my customer!"

"But if I give you money, then you need to do what I say. I will pay you anything you need for your family and for baby Tay. I'll pay for it all, but you have to come to class and finish school. You have to stop selling yourself."

At this point, we were both yelling.

The floodgates opened. "Why do you treat me this way?" she cried.

"Because you need to know who made you and what you're worth! You were not put on this earth to sell your body. Your purpose is not to sell yourself!"

Weeks passed. Two days before graduation (after two years of working with her through everything), she called me on the phone.

"Teacher, I'm done."

"Are you kidding me? You're two days away from graduation."

"I'm afraid of the success," she whispered. "If I graduate and I am out of Shear Love, I will be on my own. I would rather go back to what I know than step into the unknown."

My heart sank all the way into my stomach. All the work, care, and love we could have given her—gone. She needed to realize her worth for herself—and want it. We couldn't chase her forever.

We let her go.

Our hearts broke, but we had to do it. Six months later, she visited us again. Drugs had addled her appearance even further. She continued to sell herself—admitted she'd been pregnant again when she quit two days before graduation—and had no spark of life left in her eyes. We've not seen her in a while. She called me at the beginning of the quarantine to check in and make sure we were all safe. Later, we heard she had a fourth child and is living with a man who pays her to be his girlfriend.

Losing June was a crushing blow and a depressing lesson. No matter how bright and firm our purpose, we cannot win every time. Failure happens. It happens more certainly than success. But it doesn't mean that your purpose is wrong. It doesn't mean that you aren't capable of better.

It means it's time to pick yourself back up and keep going. Learn from it. What we learned is that we cannot want it more than them. All we can do is offer them freedom. It is up to them to take it.

Take those lessons with you into the future.

But keep going.

There Are No Failures

As cheesy as it sounds, there really are no failures. Only lessons. Sometimes they are really *big* lessons!

June's story has a yo-yo storyline that you may see in

yourself or other people. The whole experience was so up-and-down. There was never a moment when it truly stabilized. We're all like that in some regard.

Fortunately, none of the downs were failures. They were all lessons.

In the end, I look at June like the prodigal son who hasn't officially come home yet. The fact that she is still in our lives and she keeps us in her life gives me a glimmer of hope. That hope keeps me from experiencing compassion fatigue, which is when you just can't give anymore.

With situations like this, embracing the success of what you *have* done can keep you going strong. The people (like June) who slip through our fingers will still know how much we care. In fact, I've spoken to students years later who expressed that when they were at Shear Love, they knew they were loved and cared for by us and God. They differentiated between our love and the love of a Heavenly Father who also cared for them.

The amount of success that we and others have had has been a huge part of how we keep going.

To get through the mourning that can come with disappointing situations, we sometimes have to step back and look at the bigger picture. In other words, look at your successes.

How have you done well?

How have you excelled or exceeded expectations?

End your thoughts on that high note. Take the lesson, implement it, and know you'll do better with more information next time.

The same can be true for you. When you have disappointments (or what you *think* are failures), find the lesson. Let people know they're loved. Maybe the situation didn't happen the way you wanted it to, but that's okay. Everyone has a journey, and we're not in charge.

Bottom line: when something goes wrong and you think you've failed, all you have to do is find the lesson. Then it's no failure. To find that lesson, you have to be secure in yourself. After something happens, step back and ask yourself (or someone else), *Did I say everything that was necessary?*

Honestly, people tend to talk too much as it is, so you may also need to ask, *Have I done everything that I could have? Did I commit fully and give all I could in the situation?*

If so, great! You definitely haven't failed. But what can you learn from it so you do better next time? That will make things even *more* valuable to you.

You may need to ask your circle these questions as well. Has someone disappointed you on your purpose journey? Did someone not come through on something they promised? Trust me—it happens all the time! This is another great chance for you to step back and ask the five most powerful debrief questions:

1. What was I trying to do?

2. What happened?

3. What can I learn from this?

4. What should I do differently next time?

5. Now what?

Empowering Men

When I officially moved to Thailand, I arrived to support Kaylie as she started trainings and seminars for people wanting to join the fight for justice in Pattaya.[1]

It was an incredible time. We educated college-aged students about prevention, rescue, restoration, reintegration, and response. Kaylie wrote the bulk of the curriculum, while I focused on teaching reintegration.

As part of this program, we ventured into the red light district to meet some of the women there and give them an opportunity to leave. In the process, we met men there to purchase sex. We would openly and honestly talk to them. They were good discussions! The majority of them were over sixty years old.

One night, I met this guy named George at one of the bars. He was from Brooklyn, so I immediately squealed with excitement and told him that my mom is from Jersey.

He said, "Ah, so we're neighbors!"

As the conversation went on, I realized all he wanted was human connection. This was the first moment that I began to understand why these men were buying. For the workers, it was financial. For the buyers, it was an attempt to alleviate some sort of emotional craving.

George was an interesting guy, and we talked for a long time. I think you may be surprised to hear this, but he wasn't some dirty, nasty man. He was just a guy from Brooklyn who told his family he lives by the beach somewhere that's not cold.

We were laughing and having a good time, so I felt comfortable enough to probe him a bit.

"So, what are you doing here?" I asked.

"Oh, I'm retired and have money. Money goes a long way here!"

"But money goes a long way in other places too. Why *here*?"

"They're good girls, and I'm helping them out."

I understood why he thought that way. These men tend to create ideas in their head that these girls like the work. They *want* to be paid for sex.

"That's all good and well if you really think that." I paused, then said, "But can you step back for a minute and ask yourself whether this is something they want to do, or need to do?" I watched that question sink into him. The skin on his face curled together as he thought. I added, "Have you asked them if they had something else they'd rather be doing?"

He didn't answer right away. He just let it linger there.

Then George opened up to me about a Thai girl he'd really cared for. She worked at a brothel he frequented. She always made sure he was taken care of, even when he wasn't there for sex. He said she never asked for much and was always so accommodating, but unfortunately, she'd passed away.

Something about sharing that story released a wave of feelings in him. He started rambling, almost to the air, about her. Then he started to cry.

"She never asked for this! She never asked for anything! She was so kind and sweet. I knew she had a family she was taking care of. But now she's gone. And I don't know how to help anymore or who to ask."

He sat there, in complete silence, and just stared at me. It was like he was waiting for my reaction, maybe hoping I wouldn't run away. Instead, I hugged him, and when I did, I could sense that, for a moment, he felt accepted. It was truly a sweet and tender moment.

He just wanted a genuine connection with someone.

You don't need to pay for that.

My interaction with George was the catalyst for me wanting to understand buyers and the reason they do pay for sex.[2] We can use our purpose to empower others. Not only to find *their* purpose, but to live their best life.

There's so much rhetoric on empowering women these days—which is good and very needed—but we need to empower men too. If we keep empowering women, but not men, who will these women have to partner with in life?

Both men and women need to be educated and empowered simultaneously.

Planting Seeds

During another Injustice Response Training session with Kaylie and some students, we took a group of girls to the brothels to talk with the sex workers. These girls really connected with them.

When we do this, we pay pimps for the women's time. Technically, we are their customers. It's not an ideal situation, but we get access to them. In the process, we also keep them away from any men who would buy them for sex.

This particular night, we were at a bar when I spotted a man who paid for girls to come and sit with him. He wasn't the typical customer. He was attractive and in his late thirties, and was buying these girls drinks. This piqued my interest, so I went up to him, slid into the booth, and said, "Hi!" with a big grin on my face. The girl that was with him left the booth to grab something.

Nothing about me said I was there for sex. I wore a six-year-old mission T-shirt with stains on it.

Perplexed, he asked in a thick accent, "What are you doing here?"

"I live here. Where are you from?"

He explained to me that he is from Norway, but traveled to Thailand often for international business. Pattaya was always one of his main stops.

After more good conversation, I took it one step deeper. "You're a thirtysomething, attractive guy. Why are you here and not with a girlfriend back home?"

"Well, I pay for a connection. I don't have to call her tomorrow. I don't have to buy her dinner. I get what I want and leave."

"And are you getting what you want?"

He quickly snapped, "Of course I am!"

"Oh. Okay," I murmured, then added, "but you keep coming back to this place, so you must be making some kind of connection."

He nodded and described his affection for the girls in the bar. "They're kind," he said. "And so sweet."

"Those are the things you value?"

"Well, yeah! Doesn't everybody?"

"Yeah, which is why I'm asking why you're looking here and not in a genuine relationship."

He fell quiet.

The girl returned to the table. I struck up a conversation with her in what little Thai I know, which the Norwegian man couldn't understand.

"Tell me about yourself," I said in Thai.

She laid out her personal roots and reasons for her work. A tragic story, similar to many I've heard from the other women I have met in the red light district, followed.

The man tapped me on the shoulder when our discussion ended and asked me what we'd spoken about. He seemed to fear the conversation was about him. I shared her story, detailing her history. She was from a really poor village and was the main caregiver of her younger siblings. She sent everything she made back to them so they could go to school.

"The money you're about to spend on her?" I said. "It's going straight back to her siblings so they don't have to sell themselves."

Everything became very still. Maybe he realized that she was human and had a story of her own, one that he hadn't bothered to ask about. Or maybe he realized that this girl was with him for one reason only: money.

"You don't look like you're enjoying yourself anymore," I said after she left.

He remained pensive. Then, he softly said, "I never thought about it that way. I never thought that this wasn't mutual."

His words were almost lost in the chatter and noise of our environment. It was almost like he was going through a breakup.

I smiled, knowing the course of his life had just been

altered, and replied, "I know. Maybe you should think more about having a relationship that isn't manufactured. I understand that you're a businessman who travels all over the world, but you keep on coming back to these girls because you think they're waiting for you. Why wouldn't you want that from a real girlfriend or even a wife? Do you not feel worthy of being wanted and waited for at home?"

Boom! His eyes welled up with tears. "I just never thought about it that way," he said.

"Well, maybe you should start thinking about it that way."

He muttered, "Yeah, I need to go."

He quickly stood up, paid his tab, and walked out the door.

Even if he couldn't admit it, I was happy knowing that his perspective had just been changed for the better.

This is how our pursuit of purpose changes lives. Slowly. An inch at a time. Maybe that guy went to another bar to pay for another woman there, but maybe he didn't. When it comes to purpose work, we're often doing small things over time that make a big difference in the long run.

With purpose, we can empower each other and slowly—but steadily—change the world.

Not by Accident

It's always fascinating to hear how these buyers rationalize their actions. So many of them think that they're helping these women by buying sex, or that the women actually want to be there! Don't get me wrong—that's sometimes true. But most of the time, they don't have a choice.

I actually had an argument with a guy once because he

believed that the sex workers were there because they wanted to be.

"Come on," he cried, "they love this! They look so happy. They're wearing hot outfits, and they're getting tons of attention. What woman wouldn't want that?"

I pointed him in the direction of the girls in a bar across the street. I told him to look at the faces of the ones not sitting with customers. You could see the sadness written on them.

"Everything they do on the street is an act," I said. "It's part of a character they're playing. They need to make money and reach their quota of customers per night. That's all this is. It's not because they love selling their body."

The man watched as the women transformed from sullen to peppy when a few men walked by. When the men disappeared and the women returned to their glum states, he whispered, "Oh my gosh."

His entire perspective changed.

If your heart is where it is supposed to be, you won't be chasing these things. These men don't just wake up one day and think, *I'm gonna go purchase sex from a girl in a third-world country for $5, even though she'll be a stranger and won't speak my language.*

That doesn't happen!

A man doesn't just end up here by accident. They end up here for a multitude of reasons, but it usually has something to do with their own actions or behaviors, or unresolved issues from their past. Many were workaholics whose families resented them for not being around enough.

I want to note that these are not terrible men. Instead, they're men who have suffered. They've experienced pain. They likely have their own trauma that has caused them to lash out and abuse others.

After years of understanding the sex industry and its consumers, I've learned that these men have holes in their hearts. Holes that they try to fill with things like sex. They want meaning, companionship, and fulfillment, but you can't truly receive those feelings when you pay for them. It only provides temporary relief.

The truth is, they become emptier in the process.

As bizarre as it may be to hear, part of the process of helping these girls is helping these buyers. As long as men are taught to relieve their stresses and problems by outsourcing in some way, the sex industry will persist.

That's why we must empower men.

As long as there is a demand, there will be supply. When we address these holes in the hearts of men, we will see a change. That's why we focus on the buyers also, and not just those being sold. Once we establish some trust and enter their hearts, we shatter their preconceptions and show them that their actions cause harm.

We can show these men that they don't have to be
the problem. They can be the solution.

No One Wants to Be Here

Ben was abused as a kid.

In early high school, he came out as gay. His family was upset, but they saw the chance to capitalize on it. They said, "You're gay? Go to Pattaya. Since you can't have a family, you might as well have sex with men and send us the money."

They pulled him out of school and sent him away.

He wanted to be an engineer but had no economic resources. Just a dream (which is important). Let's just say that when you're a teen in Pattaya with little education and no support . . . it's not good.

For the next few years, he sold his body to men for money. Taylor and I met him when he was twenty-two, on the first night we did an outreach for men. He was so nice, polite, very intelligent, and the sweetest kid. We went back to his bar so many times that he finally asked, "Why do you keep coming here?"

"We run a program for men who don't want to be here anymore."

Ben laughed and said, "No one wants to be here! I mean, who would? Almost all the men who work here are straight. I'm not, but almost all of them are. They're just here to feed their families or pay medical bills. No one wants to be here! That's ridiculous."

"Great!" I said. "Do you want to be a barber?"

"I want to do anything except be here. Ultimately, I want to be an engineer."

"I can't teach you to build things, but I can teach you how to do a dope fade! That will let you learn a skill and make money. Give it a few years, and you can pay your way through engineering school."

He left with us that night after we staged it to look as though we were his customers. On our way out, Ben said to Taylor and me, "This is the best day of my life."

Ben graduated top of the class.

He became fluent in English and comes back to Shear Love once a week to pick up new skills so he can keep learning. He's a phenomenal barber and earned a job in a shop away from town. His clientele is loyal, and he's saving tons of money while he decides if he still wants to do engineering.

Either way, he is empowered. No one can tell him his worth or what it is based on. He is gifted, and he knows it.

FORGIVENESS IS NECESSARY

Gaining a knowledge about why men pay for sex was instrumental for me to forgive the man who abused my brother for years. It also allowed me to forgive my ex-husband. It set the foundation for me to forgive other hurts that rose from my past and unknowingly held me back.

That's why forgiveness is necessary to do purpose work. You have to forgive and let go of the things in your past or you won't achieve your full potential. It takes significant energy to deal with constant memories from the past. Not forgiving keeps us mentally enslaved. Forgiveness allows us to cut the chains, stops the reliving of the pain, and allows momentum to move forward.

Your amazing power won't be reached if you allow other people to continue to live rent-free in your mind. I could never empower men to be better if I hadn't forgiven the men who caused pain in my life. Now, I am not held back from having great relationships with the amazing men who are in my world now. I understand the *why*.

Why did certain things happen?
Why were those decisions made?
Knowing that makes it possible for me to live out my purpose more fully, and change the world.

The same is true for you.

Use the questions below to figure out what forgiveness you can extend to those who have wronged you:

1. Who do you need to forgive?

2. What's holding you back from forgiving them?

3. Are these people still in your life?

4. Is staying angry at them affecting them in any way?

5. What will happen if you forgive them?

6. What will happen if you don't forgive them?

The Restorative Process

Pursuing your purpose is tough. Not because it shifts your current life and the way you look at the world, but because it dredges stuff up that you can't ignore. There's a restorative effect for you and those you serve.

Don't Let Her Sit Down

A sweet girl named Dara came into a beauty school where I volunteered in Cambodia. She was brought from another part of the country from a safe house. At five years old, she had been smuggled into Cambodia in the back of a chicken truck from a surrounding country. A trafficker paid $90 for her, and she was enslaved in sex trafficking for close to nine years. This program was meant to be part of her therapy.

They brought Dara in for the hairstyling class and said, "She is so creative. This will be really great for her healing process and reintegration into life away from sex trafficking."

When she joined the class, we learned more about her

and got to know her. The director of the organization assisting her met with me to check on her progress and asked, "How is she doing?"

"She's hard on herself, but that's it. Otherwise, she's doing great."

He nodded. "Okay, great. Just don't let her sit down."

"Wait, what? Why can't she sit down?"

With a firmer tone, he said, "Do *not* let Dara sit down, no matter what. This is part of her therapy. She has to push through when she's having a hard time, not sit down and give up. If she does that, stand by her. Make sure she grasps the concepts when she struggles. Take her hands, work with her, and do not let her sit down or curl up in a ball on the floor."

That precise moment is when I realized that their education was part of their recovery.

Part of their restoration into a new life after so much had been taken from them.

When working with her, I did just what he said. One time, she went to a corner and tried to get into the fetal position and cry, but I pulled her up and made her stand. I stood behind her, held her up, made her work. She was the youngest and one of the best in the class, and she ended up pushing through.

These days, she still does hair, but specializes in high-end weddings for brides and bridal parties. She makes fantastic money in the bridal industry in Cambodia. The best part? She charges $90 an hour.

The same price she was sold for.

Healing Ourselves

There are things that all of us need to face and work through in order to heal from our past, whether that's getting rid of something that you do that has never really served you, getting rid of some*one* who has never served you, or going to professional counseling for the first time.

At Shear Love, we have mandatory counseling for all our workers. It came about that way because of a devious woman named Amara.

Amara taught all of us the power and depth that the restorative process requires.

Forgiving Amara

While doing an outreach event in Pattaya, two of our outreach volunteers, Dorothea and Julianne, came across a stunningly beautiful girl on the streets. She didn't seem quite typical for those circumstances, but she was certainly very scared.

They talked to her and got her contact information, and Dorothea came to me saying, "Dianna, you need to talk to her."

"Great!" I said. "Let's see if she'll meet."

Amara agreed. Immediately, when I met her over mango smoothies, I thought she was wonderful. She had the sweetest little nose and gorgeous skin that looked photoshopped. She was the definition of an African braided beauty. Her demeanor was gentle and very ladylike.

"Is it okay that you're here right now?" I asked her.

"Yes." Her eyes darted around. "For now."

"Can you tell me how you got here?"

She didn't respond.

"Do you want to be here?" I asked gently. "What can we do to help you?"

"No!" she snapped. "Do I look like I want to be here?"

Her sudden defensiveness wasn't unusual, so I just said, "I can help you get out of here."

"Please, do not call the police. My passport was stolen and I'm terrified. I know what the police have done to my friends. They are not nice to people like me!"

"Not calling the police," I said. "I'll just be calling people from our team so we can help to protect you."

While I made some calls, she watched me closely, then asked Dorothea, "Who is she talking to?"

"People who can help you get out of here."

Panic filled Amara's eyes. She stood up. "Oh. Um . . . I'm just going to run into that 7-Eleven right there and get some water, and I'll be right back."

While I watched her walk away, I had a weird feeling about this whole situation. Eventually, we went over there to find her, and she was gone. Despite text messages to reassure her she could trust us, we couldn't get her to come back. We found out her trafficker relocated her after our meeting. She accused us of being bad friends for putting her in danger.

It sent Dorothea and me into a spiral. *What did we do wrong?* I thought. *How could I have improved my approach? What step did I miss? What did I do to scare her?*

A week or two later, Amara messaged Dorothea back and said, *I'm sorry I called you a bad friend. I'm sorry I ran off. I just didn't know what else to do.*

My entire staff was elated that Amara had reached back out, so I said to Dorothea, "Don't tell her that she can trust you. Just keep being kind and let her know that if she needs help, we are here."

For three months, Amara would communicate with us on and off. Eventually, she decided to take our help. We met her really late on a Friday night after she found a bus to Pattaya. Her disheveled appearance didn't detract from her obvious happiness to see us.

"I'm so happy to see you, my sisters," she said brightly.

We arranged for her meals and safe living that weekend. Monday morning, Julianne picked up Amara, and she arrived at Shear Love in the cutest pink dress and a bright smile. I had already told our current beauty students about her situation, so as soon as she walked in, they bowed and hugged in a warm, loving welcome. They embraced her as one of their own, and some students even used their own salary to pay for her food.

My heart was thrilled by these circumstances.

To forge safety and a new life for Amara and because her passport had been stolen, we talked to several partner organizations in the area that do similar work. Annie, the director of an organization in Bangkok called Night Light, told us to go to the police, file specific forms stating the situation, and pay a small immigration fee.

Some investigators from LIFT International flew down from Chiang Mai to start the investigation into Amara's trafficker. Two detectives, Amara, Julianne, and I sat in our counseling room, which is a space designed to feel safe.

The detective said to Amara, "Tell us what you remember about your trafficker. If you leave things out, that's okay. We can always go back. Whatever you share is what we can use to stop these people from doing this to anyone else."

"Someone came to my village," she said, tears in her eyes. "They were driving a fancy car. They said they had an opportunity for me to make more money. My family urged me to go." She looked to me and Julianne for support. The expression on her face seemed to ask, *Can I do this?* As if she were trying so hard to find the strength within herself.

"You're safe," I said softly. "You can do this."

Eventually, Amara shared her coercion story. She'd been trafficked for six months before we met her. The detectives were very comforting, and they were able to draw out the traffickers' names, where they were from, and even the make and model of the car. She showed them the village on a map and said, "I don't want any other women to experience this."

We worked with LIFT to help locate the traffickers, while Night Light advised us on the immigration process for Amara. Thankfully, the day came when we were finally able to send her home.

Amara was ecstatic! She had gifts to take back to her family, and a few students even came with us to pray for her and comfort her as she was leaving.

Stephanie and I took her to the airport. The ride was such a fun, sweet time. We had all her documents, and we also had all our NGO documents to prove her story. While at the airport, we handed over all the papers to the ticket agent. The lady riffled through them, then looked at us and said, "No. She can't go. Come speak with my manager."

Panic set in.

The manager and ticket agent and I sat down. "She's illegally in this country," the manager said.

"I know," I said, but my stomach sank. Something wasn't right. "Her passport was stolen."

"No, we have records of her leaving the country months ago and no records of re-entry. She must have come in illegally. If we send her through, she will be arrested inside and not have a trial. Get her out of here. Go to Bangkok immigration immediately."

We quickly got out of there. Amara was a sobbing mess on the way back to Pattaya. She kept repeating, "I can't believe it. We did all these things, and it didn't work."

Monday morning at 5:00, we were on a bus to Bangkok immigration to clear it up. A volunteer from Night Light, Jada, came to help us with the process. She worked with the immigration process often. Once we arrived, we had to take a number and wait outside. When it came our time, they didn't allow us to go in. Amara had to go in alone, with Jada to translate.

Five minutes later, they returned with an officer who said, "We have a photo of this woman leaving through the southern border. She attempted to return and was deported. How is she here now?"

"Let me see the photo."

Amara put a hand up and said, "It's okay. You can stop now."

For several seconds, I was utterly speechless. "What?" I managed to finally say. "You want us to stop?"

Jada sent me a look and nodded. Something wasn't right. The officer took us to an interrogation area, then departed, saying, "A detective will be right in."

"What happened?" I asked Jada.

She shrugged wearily. "She's definitely in this country illegally. I saw the photo. It's true, and . . . I don't know where to take it from here."

This meant so many things that it was hard to figure it out all at once. For one thing—Amara had definitely lied to us. Her passport hadn't been stolen. Which meant that there could be other lies as well.

"Tell us what happened," I said to Amara.

She sighed, then proceeded to tell us a story about a guy from Malaysia bringing her across the border, similar to how human smugglers bring people illegally over the Mexican border.

I stopped her. "Nope. I know that could not have happened. Try again."

She said something about sneaking through customs in the airport, and I stopped her again.

"Nope. I also know that's not true."

Stephanie, who had been quiet for a lot of this, said, "We can't help you if you don't tell us the truth."

Amara attempted several more lies, each of them worse than the one before. My stomach felt sicker with each one. Finally, the detectives came back. She was being arrested for illegally entering Thailand. Stephanie and I went with Amara to the International Detention Center while Jada returned to her office. Amara sobbed in our laps on the way over.

We took her phone and other possessions, promised we'd call her sister for her, and then let her go. After that, Stephanie and I stared at each other.

"What just happened?" I asked.

A bit dazed and confused, we tried to reach Amara's sister, but she never answered. Then Stephanie started going through Amara's phone, and details came to light. Naked photos of women. Lewd text messages to customers. Amara had been messaging men the entire time she was with us.

Her whole story was a lie.

To make matters worse, Amara sent a note to me through Jada, who visited the IDC (International Detention Center) regularly to check on people there.

The note said:

Dearest Dianna,

I'm sorry you've gotten involved in this. Check my suitcase, because my passport is hidden in the lining, along with other legal documents for Ugandan women I know. They are documents that all need to be destroyed. Can you get them and destroy them? Then call my sister and tell her to book a flight home for me.

Um . . . what? She still had her passport? And her sister could afford to buy her a ticket to Africa? I was dumbfounded.

We immediately searched her suitcase and found multiple IDs for other African women. Amara had visa stamps to Thailand (including her deportation stamp) and all over Asia a number of times. She was a world traveler with more than seven phones for different customers, complete with photos, videos, and more on each.

Not only that, but we found enough incriminating evidence to suggest that she was involved in the trafficking of African women to Asia for sex.

After downloading the info from the phones, we found enough to free children from sexual exploitation and have traffickers and perpetrators arrested. Some of those children were younger than two years old. Amara has been black-listed from ever traveling to Asia again—which is a major win.

Not only that, but several major traffickers were also taken down. She may have even been the person controlling this sex-trafficking ring, although I feel she was more of a middle person giving info and trading the women.

After Amara was taken from us, it left our outreach team emotionally and physically destroyed. It was, and still has been, a difficult healing process. We were disillusioned. Set off course a bit. How had we not seen it?

How had we been so duped by someone we genuinely cared about?

Restoring Our Hearts

For several weeks, we were subdued. How do we prevent this in the future? How could she do that to us?

This is how the restorative process can happen. In our pursuit of purpose and the betterment of the world, we fall. We mess up. We're duped. Maybe we say the wrong thing at the wrong time, or we reach out to the wrong people. It may seem as if all our work has just shattered, or we don't know what we're doing after all.

But that's not true. I *know* what I'm here for—and so do you.

In purpose work, you have to stumble. To recognize that, in the loss, the light comes. Amazing things for our restorative process came out of the Amara failure. We gave freedom to several people! After mourning, we came through this stronger.

Before the Amara situation came to light, we had always strongly encouraged counseling for our workers, but now it is mandatory in order to work with us in the field. This case caused so much long-lasting damage that we pulled back from outreach for a while, and even shied away from international cases. We felt like we needed way more knowledge and wisdom before doing anything else.

The FBI contacted me as we attempted to put ourselves back together emotionally. "I want you to know," the agent said, "that these online predators will never see the light of day again because you were not afraid to dig and find the information we needed. Amara is blacklisted and can never come back to Asia. There are some pretty serious pedophiles in prison as a result of your determination. I'm proud of that, and you should be too."

Busting pedophiles always makes my day, but Amara still sat uneasily with me. What if I had been duped before? Would I be again?

One of the detectives from LIFT got on the phone with me. He said, "I have been a detective for over a decade, and that woman fooled me. Do not allow that woman to stop you from helping others."

That changed the game.

Sometimes, through the restorative process, we just need to reach back out to our community and let them give us comfort. My team and I were grateful he said that, because he eased the tension all of us could feel.

That's the thing about purpose work, however. Even if Amara herself didn't need freedom, those who had been under her power did. We still found freedom for many people, including children, who needed it.

Fighting for freedom is my purpose . . . so we're still going.

Albeit far more wisely.

Patience

P atience truly is a virtue.

Which is no less true when it comes to finding and fulfilling your purpose. Social media, Wi-Fi, and modern life has made us *so* impatient. We want everything to happen the very moment we think about it. We don't really know how to slow down and wait anymore. It's like everything needs to be microwaved, when most things should be baked to taste the best. I learned that from my Stephanies!

Obviously, a real pizza tastes better than a hot pocket!

When it comes to your purpose, sometimes you have to wait in order for the best path to manifest. Sometimes you have to be patient with the people who would be easier to let go of. Sometimes, you have to be the *most* patient with yourself as you learn and stumble your way through this work.

Even when it's so hard.

CHANNA

Channa was a woman I almost didn't accept into the Shear Love program in Thailand.

When I first met her for an interview, she had so much attitude. I literally said to Kelli afterward, "No. We're not accepting this girl. I want people who want help to come to this program. She clearly doesn't want it."

P Fon, a woman rescued from the brothels by our partners at Tamar Center, was involved in the situation with Channa. P Fon called me, and we talked in somewhat-broken English, as P Fon spoke mostly Thai.

"I know that you have talked with Channa, but she has not received a callback. I want to know where you are at with her application."

"We're pretty close to a full class," I said. "We have spots left, but I don't know if I'll give one to her. She wasn't serious. She would not look me in the eye during the interview. She was dismissive, aloof, blasé, and didn't care about anything. She does not seem like she wants to do this."

P Fon pleaded with me, "Promise me you'll give her a chance."

"Honestly, P Fon, I don't know if I want to. It wouldn't be fair to all the other girls who *really* want to be here."

"Please try. She has children and needs to get out of this life. Promise me you'll give her one chance."

Of course, I respect P Fon so much that I did it. I let Channa in—but I was not having it. If she gave us problems, I was ready to kick her out the first week.

After Channa learned that we'd accepted her, she went back to P Fon and said, "They said I could come to the class but that I can not take any customers."

P Fon said, "Yes, isn't it amazing? During the program,

they will give you a salary so you can learn, and you never have to go back to that life again."

"What do I care?" Channa shrugged. "I can go take customers and make more money if I want to."

"If that's what you want to do," P Fon said, "then don't waste Dianna and Shear Love's time. The only reason you have this position is because I fought for you. I'm the one who is sticking up for you. If you waste Dianna's time, that looks bad on me. Do not do that."

Despite being somewhat frightened after talking to P Fon, Channa came to the first day, quiet and morose. As I watched her in class, it seemed even more incredible that one of the other girls in the class was her sister. Channa's sister was ready to go, excited, and wanted it so badly.

"I'm never going back!" she declared that first day.

Channa stayed quiet.

Kelli—our lead educator in Thailand—took all the girls to the STI clinic for testing. That year, we had fifteen girls in the class and none of them had ever been checked. Kelli sat down, signed them all in, and waited there until each girl had received her results. Channa was halfway down the list (about seventh in line).

"Why are you here?" Channa asked Kelli.

Kelli blinked. "Well, I'm here to make sure all of you are okay."

"No, but why are you *here*? You don't have to stay here. We can all handle this by ourselves. You don't have to wait."

"Of course I do!" Kelli said with a smile. "I want to make sure that you're cared for. This is a very scary moment, and I'm here to support you."

Channa was so confused by Kelli's response that she just sat there and stared for a moment. The whole idea that Kelli cared enough to stay for hours in this clinic perplexed

Channa. Of course, Kelli stayed until the last girl got her results. Even then, Channa couldn't believe it.

With that, she started to see that Shear Love was different. We actually cared.

As time passed, she seemed happier in class. She would participate more. Three or four months in, she confided in Kelli. "I almost didn't accept your offer to be in the class. I was going to keep taking customers, but I didn't because I realized you actually care for me. You really care for these girls. Also, I'm really scared of Dianna, and I thought if she found out, she'd kill me!"

Kelli laughed and said, "Well, she'd definitely be upset! Thank you for your honesty. I'm so happy you are still here."

Not only that, but more of Channa's story eventually came out. She'd been married to an extremely abusive man who left her with nothing but the children. They needed to eat, which had forced her to work in the red light district.

In the end, Channa graduated top of her class. She proved herself to be one of the most phenomenal stylists we've seen. Her story reminds me all the time that with a little patience and a lot of love, our purpose work can take us on paths we never saw coming.

Your own purpose work will require patience from you in different ways. Be ready to sink into it. Be ready to let go of control, trust in others, and allow the path to appear. It's okay to wait a little bit. To work with people (or yourself) with more patience than you'd normally expect.

Not so coincidentally, Channa was the girl I called as soon as COVID started. I said to her, "You know how to crochet. I'll pay you to come teach other women how to knit so they can have work during COVID."

Her immediate response?

"I'm there. And can I bring some of the friends I worked with back in the bars? I know they need work."

Channa came back to Shear Love the next morning, went with Stephanie to purchase the yarn and supplies, and started the class two days later. She's now working with Shear Love and Sew Free full time. Now, it's Channa who takes the girls to the clinic for STI testing. She is the one praying for their strength and dignity. She encourages them in this new life.

Channa has started to find *her* purpose.

All because of a little bit of patience.

Her journey has been truly amazing. We've seen her go from a bratty, frightened girl to a woman who empowered herself and changed her own life. She's the lead teacher of our sewing class. She prays with these women, loves them, and cares for them. She teaches new knitting and crochet techniques and keeps a flawless inventory. Her transformation still stuns me.

By the way, *Channa* means *victory*.

LET IT RAIN

Summer of 2015 was the first time Kaylie and I went together to the red light district while running an injustice training course in Pattaya. The course required classroom time and fieldwork. Fieldwork meant we went to the red light district to meet sex workers. Becoming their friend is usually the first step.

It was 10:00 p.m. and hot as a Southern summer day—100°F with 100% humidity. Thailand is disgustingly hot. We first went to Section 6, the most infamous part of the red light district. On any given night, Section 6 has anywhere from 1,500 to 2,000 women for sale. It's the length of a New York City block.

And it's absolutely horrible.

The women all appear to be depressed, scared, high, or drunk. The pain is etched on their faces. None of them want to be there.

While in Section 6, Kaylie and I saw a strikingly beautiful girl. She was a little heavier, which is unusual for a Thai girl. Her skin was rich, dark, and warm. I thought she may have been part Indian with her brown, flawless skin and bright eyes. Her ebony hair fell to her waist, half-hiding a risqué outfit.

She was gentle and quiet. Guarded and soft. She didn't fit any stereotype. She also spoke great English, so we were able to have a conversation. Her name was Rain.[1]

Kaylie and I paid to sit down to talk with her.

We immediately loved her. After that night, we went to see her every Thursday. Eventually, she started to look for us with excitement. We built a sweet, amazing friendship with her. She giggled like a six-year-old, and we couldn't get enough. We learned that she'd purposely gained weight in hopes that men would be repulsed by her and not want to buy her for sex. We became more and more determined to get Rain help.

One night, she finally asked us, "Why are you here? It's not for sex, right?"

"No, we're not here for sex."

"Then why?"

Kaylie said, "Well, we're visiting. We've gotten to know you and enjoy spending time with you."

"Well, I've enjoyed spending time with you."

Our friendship continued, slow and steady. Eventually, it

came time for Kaylie to go back home to the US. Before she left, Kaylie told me, "Free Rain. Get her out, whatever it takes!"

No pressure, or anything.

For the next six months, I went every week to talk to Rain. We just chatted about life. It got to the point that customers were teasing her about it. At one point, a guy said to her, "Come on! Let's go already."

In a dead-serious tone, she told him, "I'm with a customer right now. You can find someone else."

That's when I realized she was starting to see her inestimable worth.

In December, I told her, "Listen, I've already told you about it, but I'm starting that beauty school in January. The whole point is to help women who are in your situation."

"I know you are."

"I want to offer you a way out of this. I can promise you a place to live and an awesome education, and that you'll be surrounded by people who love and care for you. You can work in any salon in Thailand after this. You'll never have to be in the red light district again. You're worth far more than what anyone here can pay."

She sat there with her eyes bugging out of her head. Eventually, she said, "I have to think about this."

"I'll be back next week, and you have my number. Just think it over."

She promised to think about it, bowed to me, and led me out. Kaylie and I prayed like crazy.

Rain called me on Christmas Eve and asked if we could meet for breakfast. As a Buddhist, she doesn't celebrate Christmas. Me? I'm all over Christmas breakfast!

"Heck yeah," I said.

We met at a little café. "I really want to come," Rain said, poking at her food. "I *need* to come. My body hurts. But more than that, my soul hurts. I need you to help me. But I'm going to spend time with family first. I need to get things in order there before I can be present here."

"Of course," I said. "We'll take care of you, Rain."

Rain was the first student we enrolled.

She graduated a year later. She did hair and worked at a market to save money. Two years ago, she bought ten acres of land in the north for her mother and built a small hut and a place to grow crops.

When she told me all her wonderful updates, I asked, "Now what?"

"I'm working hard to save money to build a salon there. It would be the only salon in the village. Right now, people have to go into town for their hair needs."

With tears in my eyes, I said, "I'm so flippin' proud, you have no idea. Remember how we went through budgeting in class?"

"Yes."

"What is your budget? Did you get that in order?"

"Yes! I know the amount I need."

"Bring it in. I'll see what Shear Love can do to help you."

With a proud smile, she said, "Thank you, but no. I can do this on my own."

This is what I want! I love to see people stand on their own two feet and be able to function on their own. It's an amazing feeling to not be wanted or needed. Through patiently visiting her, we fostered an independence in her that no one can take. This is the exact reason we named our organization after her.

She is happily married to a man who respects her, has a baby girl, and is doing amazing now—living her best life.[2]

STRATEGY AND PATIENCE

You can't fly by the seat of your pants in fulfilling your purpose. You may like to try, but you probably won't come out the victor. There's an element of strategy and patience that has to be in place for this to happen well. This is something I've learned extensively from the chairman of our board, Joe Vargas.[2] As a retired police captain, Joe knows firsthand what it takes to create a successful strategy to bring down the bad guys!

There's no cowboy rescue, either. You can't just rush into a problem, guns blazing, ready for something to happen. Believe me. I've tried! That method isn't planned, and that's a problem.

You must have patience.

A lot of organizations say, "We are here for the one." But when it comes to "the one," they often neglect the twenty who also need help. Sometimes, you have to be patient, let one person go for a little while, and develop a plan to save twenty plus the one. Maybe that sounds logical enough. Maybe it even sounds simple.

But it isn't always that easy.

That's a difficult stance, and it's also a moral stance. In your purpose work, be prepared to wait. Observe. Let the path reveal itself. Then you can build a good strategy and rely on your plan. Using strategy over a shotgun, I-will-save-this-struggling-person has proven better for us multiple times.

On Valentine's Day in 2019, there was a fourteen-year-old transgender girl who wore red lipstick but still looked like a boy. He was transitioned to a girl against his wishes by his family, and preferred the he/him pronouns. Our outreach team spoke with him, then we worked with another high-profile rescue group for help.

We discreetly followed him back to the bar where he said he worked, and we sent men posing as buyers to talk with him to get more information.

Although we wanted to save him right there, we waited. We needed to get a little farther.

Because we held off, we were able to help eleven other boys that were younger than him in his same situation, locked in the rooms above the bar. We shut down an entire ring.

We helped one *and* took down a system with patience, a plan, and a strategy. That is victory, even though it feels like agony because it takes a while. It took far more time than we wanted it to, but it was worth it, especially to the other eleven boys.

Step back, look at your situation, and act accordingly.

ISABELLA

Isabella lived in Mexico with an abusive husband and her children. She started attending beauty classes in 2011, after she had found us.

The fighting between her and her husband had become so bad that her classmates supported, prayed, and helped as best as they could. They told her, "Amiga, get out of this toxic relationship!"

She didn't. At least, not right away.

One day, later in the year, she came to school with a broken nose that was all bandaged up. Her husband had taken out his rage on her once again.

Beth, the hairstylist who built the school there, ran to Isabella in a panic. The rest of her classmates followed and were equally as concerned. Near tears, Beth quickly ushered her into the classroom and asked, "What happened?"

Isabella quietly responded, "Dinner wasn't ready on time."

Out of complete shock, Beth stared at her, speechless. Another student spoke up and said, "Yeah, you should've had dinner ready on time."

More of the students began nodding their heads in agreement. Still in shock, Beth said, "Everyone sit down! We need to talk."

The students sat down as they gently tended to Isabella's wounds. Beth began, "I don't care if dinner was five hours late, that gives your husband no right to hit you!"

Now the *students* were speechless.

Beth continued, "None of you deserves to be treated this way. Ever. I will not stand by and watch you, my sweet girls, be treated like this."

The ladies sat down, dumbfounded.

These women were so used to being treated this way that they could hardly understand it *wasn't* their fault. The words coming from Beth were foreign, yet comforting. Hearing the person they had looked up to for so long tell them how much they mattered was a relief.

Yet these women continually go back to these domestically violent homes daily.

And Isabella was still going home to that same abusive house.

This is common in the abusive relationships we see worldwide. Stockholm syndrome is a very real thing. (Stockholm syndrome is where you come to love and care for your abuser.) My brother experienced it with the man who abused him.

After an hour of Beth trying desperately to reach them

about their worth, Isabella began to understand the depth of her value. She finally gathered the inner strength to leave her situation and bring her and her children to safety.

But until she did that, man, was it frustrating.

I couldn't believe it took Isabella's husband breaking her nose to get her out of the situation. But then I think back to my abusive marriage—it took me a long time to leave, too. Now, I'm so grateful to have that experience and insight.

As a result of her newfound self-worth, Isabella is now married to a wonderfully supportive husband who loves her and treats her with so much respect. Nine months to the day after their wedding she gave birth to a beautiful baby girl. I saw her days before she delivered and I had never seen her more full of joy. Isabella now owns a salon in town where she employs graduates from the beauty school program.

My purpose requires patience of me constantly because I so badly want better things for people. It's painful to watch others go through hell, because I know what freedom feels like. I know what it feels like to be free on the other side. I know what it's like to walk through the light at the other end of the tunnel. But they have to want it for themselves.

And sometimes that waiting is the hardest part.

But when they learn it for themselves—there's no denying that it was worth the wait.

Live Your Legacy Now

Now that you've come this far in identifying and working through your purpose, let's talk about why this all *really* matters.

Why work so hard for your purpose? Billions of people never even think about their purpose. So why should you?

Because you want to be joyful and make an impact. You want to deepen your experience. You want to become the best version of yourself.

You want to change the world.

All of that comes down to your legacy. To everything you will leave behind when you die. Your deathbed is not the time to think about your legacy. Right *now* is the time to think about it.

In fact, you need to live your legacy now.

If you're not willing to do it now, you won't do it then (whenever "then" is). Besides, when you've hit your deathbed, it's already too late. In the famous words of Lin-Manuel Miranda in the production *Hamilton*, legacy is, "Planting seeds in a garden you will never see."

I disagree. Why would you keep doing this if you never saw *any* results?

What if you *could* see those seeds take root and bloom?

What if you could see the sweet fruit of your hard labor?

I can easily say I have absolutely seen fruit, plants, flowers, and trees grow in front of me as a result of my work. It happens. When I live my legacy, it blooms like a garden, and I enjoy it as much as anyone.

Talk about creating a powerhouse to fuel your purpose.

OBSERVE IT NOW

Julianne met Tee on Beach Road one night during outreach.

He stood on the street, waiting for a man to walk up and bargain a price for him for the night. In those moments where he felt so low and deep in depression, he wondered how this had become his life.

Julianne (aka, the ray of sunshine) walked up with a bright smile and asked if he needed help. She handed him a package of condoms with a note hidden inside that read in Thai, "If you need help, please call."

He responded immediately, "You can help me?"

"Yes, we can," Julianne smiled.

Tee exclaimed, "Help me now! I don't want to call later. I want you to help me now!"

Julianne took him to McDonalds for ice cream with a few members of the Crossroads team. They talked to him in-depth about his life and how he'd ended up on the streets. The next morning, she brought him to Shear Love. I interviewed him and accepted him into our barber program on the spot. He was in tears, beyond grateful for this opportunity. For a while, he stood in disbelief that he never had to go back to that way of life.

Tee graduated from the Shear Love barber class more than two years ago. He now works for us as an instructor teaching hair and English. He worked as hard as he possibly could to improve his vocational skills and his language skills to now give others the same opportunity he was given years ago.

That is living legacy.

Five Biggest Regrets

Australian nurse Bronnie Ware worked in palliative care with people who were actively dying. She asked each person on their deathbed about their biggest regrets.

Here are the top five things they wished they'd done differently:

1. Had courage to live a life for themselves rather than for what other people expected. People realized how many of their dreams had died because of doing what others expected.
2. Spent less time working. They wished they'd spent more time in relationships that had meaning.
3. Found the tenacity to express their feelings. Many people are afraid of what others may think or say, or of consequences if they speak up. They end up resenting themselves for their silence.
4. Stayed in touch with friends better. They felt they put money and work over their friendships too often.
5. Let themselves be happier.

The words *happening* and *happier* derive from similar roots, and I don't think that's a mistake. The question that follows is this: What were these people not allowing to happen in their lives that would have made them feel happier?

What did they do (or not do) that led to less fulfillment?

We should ask ourselves the same questions, and we should do it often. If it's fulfillment you're seeking, purpose will help you find it. But just like with June, we have to choose to be happy. Many people don't realize that happiness is a choice. So is sadness.

If you put yourself in miserable situations, you're going to be miserable.

Living your legacy is a choice you can make right now.

Dee Jai

When Dee Jai was eleven years old, her mother prostituted her on the beaches of Pattaya. Her mother was on drugs and not in her right mind as she rotated through tons of boyfriends.[1]

At the time, Dee Jai was being sexually abused by one of the boyfriends. Her mom found out, became jealous, and sold her daughter to her drug dealer. The drug dealer kept her captive as his personal sex slave when she was twelve years old.

At thirteen, she had her first son.

At fourteen, she had her second son.

People in the village started to notice that something wasn't right. The police came over and said, "You're a child —you shouldn't be having kids."

The government took her kids (ages one and two at the

time) and put them in a different home, then arrested the man. While in some ways it was an exciting development because that sort of justice just doesn't happen here, it broke Dee Jai's heart.

Dee Jai was fifteen at that point. She couldn't go back to her mom, so she went straight into the brothels. She took herself right to the red light district.

At nineteen or twenty years old, she became pregnant again, by a man who paid to have sex with her. So desperate not to have another baby, she went to a back-alley abortion clinic, which is beyond illegal in Thailand. You cannot have an abortion at any stage of pregnancy. During the sonogram before the abortion, Dee Jai heard her daughter's heartbeat. She left. She couldn't do it.

From there, Tamar Center found her. They sent an outreach team into the brothel where she worked and brought her into their training program. They gave her counseling, spiritual mentoring, and lessons about hygiene. They noticed she was really good at hair, then called me.

Dee Jai came to our program and was a phenomenal student. She won nearly every hair contest in school. She also struggled heavily with depression because she had gained over 100 pounds. If she was heavy, then men wouldn't like her, she reasoned. It was an intentional way to protect herself. At one point during the school year, she broke a chair in class after sitting in it.

"I want to be healthy and lose weight," she said, "but I'm not motivated."

"You have one of two options," I replied. "One, you pay for this chair to be fixed. Two, you and I start working out together every day at lunch and I will pay for the chair to be fixed."

Every day for the next six or seven months, Stephanie,

Dee Jai, and I walked, swam, climbed stairs, and lifted weights. The very first day we worked out, Dee Jai sweated like crazy, cried, and panted.

By the end of the year, she'd lost thirty kilos (over sixty pounds).

"I used to have nightmares of Dianna saying, 'Come on, come on, come on!'" she said during her speech at graduation. "But now, look where I'm at. I'm only here because you pushed me. I'm only here because you helped me get here."

Dee Jai had her government ceremony to get her official license to be a hairstylist in the fall of 2020. In Thailand, it's a big deal when you receive a trade or vocational license (whether it's as a hairstylist, welder, electrician, or something else). The governor of the province comes down and hands you the certificate, and you receive a picture with him.

Tamar Center and all the staff at Shear Love attended.

Dee Jai looked into the distance one night as she spoke with Ashley, Tamar's outreach leader. "Can you believe it?" she asked quietly. "It's a miracle that, years ago, I was just some little girl sleeping on the beach, hoping to earn a dollar for my mom. Now, look where I'm at."

All three of her kids live with her now.

She is the ultimate legacy story. She is *living* her own legacy. Not only do I get to see my legacy through her, but I have the honor of watching her legacy unfold through her children. Her two boys and her little girl saw their mom come out of that world.

Now they will never have to live in it.

All three kids are in school because she has a job in a good salon. She can afford to put them through school without prostituting herself.

Fully Embrace Your Purpose

Purpose, passion, and legacy all start at home with you. You cannot fully embrace your journey or your path until you deal with the demons rattling in your closet.

Give life to the people in your life.

In other words, forgive. Work through the issues there. It's hard. I get it. I've also had to work through issues with family members and friends before I could fully embrace my purpose. If you live in regret and resentment, how can you help others to leave theirs behind?

If you're miserable and sullen, how can you chase a positive action?

When you have lined up your mind, your heart, and your home, your purpose and the legacy that flows from it will follow.

Don't Wait Until You Die

In your quest to define your legacy, here are some questions to consider:

1. What keeps you stuck?

2. Why do you *go through the motions*?

3. If you were at the end of your life right now, what would you regret?

Purpose work isn't easy, but it's worth it, because you can see the fruits of your work before your eyes if you choose to live your legacy now.

Do you want to live your legacy?
Do you want to see your legacy garden grow?
(The answer is yes—you absolutely do!)

I want to leave you with one last question:

Are you the hammer—or are you the shoe?
If you're the hammer, then go out, change the world, and **be the hammer.**

Afterword

EDUCATE SURVIVORS | EQUIP FIGHTERS

To Support Shear Love

Shear Love International trains people from all walks of life. Whether they're coming from a background of poverty, abuse, exploitation, or trafficking, we believe all people deserve an education and an opportunity to succeed.

Shear Love is designed to educate and empower men and women by providing an education in hair design. Equipping people with vocational knowledge in beauty and barbering, financial training, and personal development will give them an opportunity to support their families in a dignified way.

If you're interested in supporting Shear Love as we continue our fight for freedom from sex trafficking, labor trafficking, and extreme poverty, please visit shearloveinternational.org.

To Support Sew Free

Sew Free is designed to educate and empower rescued women by providing an education in textile arts. Equipping women with vocational knowledge, financial training, and personal development will give them an opportunity to support their families in a dignified way. Our full-spectrum, faith-based, educational sewing program will give them an escape from exploitation, the chance to succeed, and the ability to focus forward on their future.

If you're interested in supporting Sew Free as we continue our fight for freedom from sex trafficking, please visit sewfree.org.

To Train Through Injustice Response

Injustice Response Training exists to equip individuals to understand how to utilize their skill sets to aid in the rescue and restoration of those in need.

Our training programs are structured and formed to each person's calling and purpose uniquely. Begin fighting injustice through our multifaceted online educational courses. Accessible anywhere on earth, you can train online to become a passionate justice seeker and effectively join the fight.

If you're interested in becoming trained in the fight for freedom and justice, please visit injusticeresponse.org.

Acknowledgments

There are too many people who have supported this book as it has come to fruition, so I will do my best to give them the acknowledgment they deserve.

Mom, thank you for your constant support of all the work I've done worldwide, even though you weren't always happy with me going. Thank you for taking so much care in shipping every shirt and beanie for Shear Love and Sew Free.

Dad, thank you for always calling me with your forehead to check that I'm still alive!

VJ, thank you for encouraging me to go, and go quickly.

Grandma Elvia, who didn't get to see this book finished, but would have considered it to be the world's greatest literary masterpiece. This and anything written about the wardrobe of Lady Diana (the actual Lady D!). Grandma would have likely said something like, "Mija, dis es so beautiful! I yam berry proud ob chu. And chu luk so perdy on de cober! Now chu need tu com home and get married and hab babies, okay? Okay!"

Master Kaylie Renee Wilson Housewright, thank you for being my partner in anti-crime, my co-founder, my sounding board, and sender of the greatest memes. I love you more than Western toilets!

My Shear Love Family

- **Stephanie,** for being the forever string to my overinflated balloon.
- **Jamie,** for dope fades, sweet video skills, and low-key hilarity.

- **Kelli,** for your dedication to every single beauty student, past, present, and future.
- **Dorothea,** aka Dodo, aka Dory, aka Dorthesha, for your artistry and your serenity.
- **Julianne,** for sunshine and your hype.
- **Sara,** for your talent and your humility.
- **Krista,** for your wise counsel.
- **Alex,** for your sweet tech skills and your Mexican memes.

My Thai family, who I couldn't accomplish this work without . . . Gideon, Goo, Aor, Nid, Aiden, Golf, Somjit, Aom, Nee, Canaan, Tiya, Prix, and Khun Tae.

My circle . . . Karissa, Celeste, Allie, Megan, Brianna, Missy, Rose, Stephanie, Posie, Ashley, Amy, Jenn, Christian, Ruth, Tiffany, Constance, Deneen, Jessica, Angela, Jon, Kathy, Renna, Jonathan, Joey, Ellice, Luc, and Stacy.

And within my circle, **my mentors** . . . Fayanna, Debbie, Lisa, Pam, Chuck, Joanna, Leanne, Karen, Joe, Jennifer, Kristi, Barb, Geza, Nella, Stan, Ted, Beth, Debbie, Terry, Steve, Shannon, Cyndi, Dr. Dave, and Candace.

My writing team, who has given more time, attention, energy, and love to this project than I ever could have asked for . . . Katie, Kristen, Kate, and Kim.

And finally, **my church family** at Crossroads, who have supported, encouraged, and loved me right from the very start of this crazy journey. I wouldn't be where I am without you guys!

Notes

Chapter 1

1. Throughout this book, I will share with you more about the survivors we help and the work we do at Free Rain through videos we have made. Let this inspire you to see just how far your purpose can take you. Directed by Nick Worrell, this film shares the heart of Shear Love: bit.ly/shearlovesmiles

Chapter 4

1. Filmed by Dorothea Schulz, the vlog shares the reality of the lockdown of the red light district of Thailand. To learn more about the red light lockdown, visit: bit.ly/redlightvlog
2. Filmed by Dorothea Schulz, this film highlights the start of Free Rain's newest vocational program, Sew Free. To learn more about our vocational program Sew Free, visit: bit.ly/sewfreefilm

Chapter 6

1. Directed by PJ Acceturo, this short film follows the story of a young woman who was rescued from Section 6: bit.ly/thesectionsixfilm

Chapter 7

1. Kelli Martin gives an emotional account of her time exploring and serving in India. To learn more about Kelli, visit: bit.ly/panoramakelli
2. Julianne Kowalski opens up about her calling to reach those forced to sell themselves in the red light districts. To learn more about Julianne, visit: bit.ly/panoramajulianne
3. In this film directed by Sidney Diongzon, Dianna Bautista recounts her experience in Kenya. For more information on my experience there, please see this film created by Sidney Diongzon: bit.ly/filmjournal9

4. Leanne Ellis recalls an intimate story of her first encounter with missions in Thailand. To learn more about Mama Lea, visit: bit.ly/panoramaleanne
5. Filmed by Ricky Dorn, Kenyan beauty instructor Carol Njua updates the progress on the beauty programs. To learn more, visit: bit.ly/shearlovemohi

Chapter 9

1. Learn more about Injustice Response Training at injusticeresponse.org
2. Kaylie Housewright and Dianna Bautista discuss the importance of empowering men in the fight against trafficking: bit.ly/FRempoweringmen

Chapter 11

1. Filmed by Dorothea Schulz, this is the story of Rain: bit.ly/RainFilm
2. Free Rain Chairman Joe Vargas gives his perspective on exploitation in Thailand. To learn more from Joe, please visit: bit.ly/panoramajoe

Chapter 12

1. Filmed by Dorothea Schulz, Dee Jai vulnerably shares her testimony and her triumph: bit.ly/freedomfoundcomplete